How To Improve Your Life

Dreams, Self-Therapy, & Genetics

By James L. Atwell

Genetic Research, LLC

The opinions expressed in this manuscript are solely the opinions of the author and do not represent the opinions or thoughts of the publisher. The author has represented and warranted full ownership and/or legal right to publish all the materials in this book.

How To Improve Your Life
Dreams, Self-Therapy and Genetics
All Rights Reserved.
Copyright © 2016 James L. Atwell
v3.0

Cover Photo © 2016 www.istockphoto.com/IgorZhurazlov with Cover Design by Elvis Chung . All rights reserved - used with permission.

This book may not be reproduced, transmitted, or stored in whole or in part by any means, including graphic, electronic, or mechanical without the express written consent of the publisher except in the case of brief quotations embodied in critical articles and reviews.

Genetic Research, LLC

ISBN: 978-0-578-17732-8

PRINTED IN THE UNITED STATES OF AMERICA

Table of Contents

Introduction i

1   A Little About the Brain and Neurogenesis 1
2   The Physiology of Sleep and Dreaming 12
3   Remembering Dreams 26
4   The Evolution of Dream Theory 37
5   Iroquoi 44
6   Temiar Senoi 47
7   Sigmund Freud 55
8   Carl Jung 66
9   B. F. Skinner 68
10 Transactional Analysis 70
11 Carl Rogers 72
12 Fritz Perls 74
13 My View of Gestalt Therapy 77
14 My Approach to Therapy 83
15 My Approach to Dreams 85
16 How to Use Dreams in Therapy 89
17 Dream Therapy in Groups 94
18 How to Use Dreams to Facilitate Counseling a Couple .. 127

19 How to Use Dreams to Facilitate Counseling Children...130
20 How to Use Dreams to Facilitate Counseling a Family...135
21 Dream Now..137
22 Conslusion About Dreams 141
23 Self-Therapy...144
24 Self-Therapy Techniques 146
25 Genetics 151
26 A Few Ways to Improve Your Life...............................164
27 The Definition of Behavior...168
28 A Little About the Past and the Future 177

Thank You..181
Bibliography 182

Introduction

You can improve your life using a few techniques in this book. In fact, there are many ways to improve a person's life. However, many people have trouble seeing any of the many ways to improve their life. This is usually because the person has so much invested in the way their life is now. It is sometimes hard to admit that my life is exactly the way I want it to be. Most of us want our lives to be different. We blame others, as though we are simply going along with what everyone else wants us to do. Many people blame money as the reason for their lives being so miserable. If they had some money, their life would be very different. If that is so, what are you willing to do to get more money? I am not talking about robbing a bank. I am talking about going back to school and getting a degree which will allow you to get a higher paying job or at least a job that you will enjoy more than any job you have ever had before. College degrees are extremely important, increase income, and help fulfill people's dreams.

Dreams are also extremely important. Not only is my life affected by my dreams, but my life is also affected by other people's dreams. With strong opinions about the importance of dreams, I learned all I could about dreams and dreaming. During the last forty years I have read everything I can find about dreams, dreaming, and sleep. I also studied my own dreams and learned to create my dreams exactly the way I want them to be.

Freud (1952, 1965) and Jung (1965) both believed dreams to be very important. Fritz Perls (1969) even believed that a person could get through the "whole cure or maturation," by fully working with every part of only one dream. Francis Mott (1977) believes that world transformation is imminent with the application of the Experimental Method of Science to the study of dreams.

There are many different beliefs in the United States about dreams, ranging from the theory that they are meaningless to a conviction that dreams are messages from God (Cayce 1962). Many people are neurotic about their dreams. By neurotic, I mean that they want their dreams to be different than they are. A study by Jersild indicates that most people would choose not to dream if given a choice (O'Nell 1976).

I held six basic beliefs when I started studying dreams and dreaming:

1.
I am controlled by an unconscious that I know nothing about.
2.
Psychotherapy is the process of finding out what is in the unconscious.
3.
During sleep, unconscious thoughts become dreams.

4.
By studying dreams I would be studying the unconscious.
5.
I have no control over my dreams; I can only observe them.
6.
I dream very seldom.

After a thorough study of the literature, I learned that all six of my beliefs were false. I therefore concluded that to become a proficient psychotherapist, it was essential for me to master the subject of dreams.

After receiving my master of arts degree in counseling psychology from Goddard College, I became very interested in using my dreams for self-therapy and finding other techniques and styles of self-therapy. Possibly, all therapy is self-therapy, in the same way that all hypnosis is self-hypnosis.

While teaching psychology at Platt College Los Angeles, I have become obsessed with studying both genetics and neurogenesis, the creation of new nerve cells in the adult human brain. There are many ways to increase neurogenesis and even more ways to destroy neurogenesis. Although most behavior is genetic, I can still change my life with the choices I make. When and how I die is determined by my genes. However, I can be killed or I can add ten to fifteen years to my life by making the correct choices. What can I change about my life to ensure that I will be more intelligent at age one hundred than I am now? If caffeine prevents neurogenesis, can I permanently give up all caffeine? I gave up eating hamburgers in 1975 and I have not eaten beef or pork for many years. After being a vegan for many years, I am now eating a little chicken and turkey. Should I once again give up chicken and turkey? It's not easy. At age seventy-one, I believe it will be easier for me to give up caffeine than it will be for me to start jogging.

1
A Little About the Brain and Neurogenesis

The average human brain contains about one hundred billion nerve cells or neurons and also contains about one trillion glia or glial cells. Rudolf Virchow, a German pathologist, is the one who named them glia, the Greek word for glue, in 1856, believing them to be passively holding neurons in place like glue (Zimmer 2009). Anyway, the neurons are specialized to receive and transmit information with chemicals and they vary in size and shape. Sensory neurons carry information to the brain and spinal cord. Motor neurons carry information away from the brain and spinal cord. Every nerve cell contains a nucleus with a complete set of chromosomes and genes. One end has a long axon with many terminal buttons. The other end has many dendrites surrounding the nucleus. The dendrites grow out and search for the terminal buttons of other nerve cells while the terminal buttons grow out and search for dendrites (Morris and Maisto 2010).

Most axons are covered with a myelin sheath made of glial cells, which serve as insulation to protect the axon from being touched by dendrites of other neurons, hold the neurons in place, and somehow speed up the chemicals traveling down the axon (Morris and Maisto 2010).

Dendrites collect information from the terminal buttons of other neurons and transmit that information to the nucleus. This collecting and transmitting of information is all done with chemicals called neurotransmitters. There are possibly a thousand different chemicals involved. Only a few of these chemicals have been studied, while nothing is known about most of them. Those few neurotransmitters that have been analyzed are almost chemically identical to illegal drugs. These chemicals move in and out of the neuron through tiny pours in the cell walls while traveling down the axon. When they reach the terminal buttons they move across the space between the terminal buttons and dendrites the same way. That space is called the synapse. When the chemical reaction reaches the dendrites, it continues down the dendrite to the cell body. The cell body collects chemicals from all the dendrites until it has received its full potential. It will not fire until it reaches its full potential. When that point is reached, it fires 100 percent of its potential down the axon. By fire, I mean it releases 100 percent of its chemical reaction inside and outside of its axon, moving downward toward its terminal buttons. This movement down the axon is called a neural impulse. The speed of the neural impulse varies from three feet per second to as fast as four hundred feet per second (Morris and Maisto 2010).

Neurons are surrounded by glial cells, which hold the

neurons in place, give the neurons all the nutrients and chemicals that they need, and take away excess chemicals that they no longer need. These glial cells make contact with the blood; the neurons do not make contact with the blood (Morris and Maisto 2010). Glial cells also play an important role in neuron regeneration, learning, and memory (af Bjerken, Marschinke, and Stromberg 2008; Cambras, Lopez, and Arias 2005; Featherstone, Fleming, and Ivy 2000; Wan et al. 2008).

Researchers now believe that glial cells are far more important than neurons. There are ten times more glial cells than neurons and they communicate with each other using calcium impulses. When a person is high on marijuana and forgets what they are talking about midsentence, the glial cells are responsible. This indicates that they have something to do with short-term memory. There are several different kinds of glia cells and they seem to be able to change into whichever kind is needed (Zimmer 2009).

In the brains of human embryos, glial cells follow their genetic instructions by stretching out tentacles and grabbing hold of each other to form a scaffolding and guide and hold the neurons in their final location (Zimmer 2009). Starting at about age three, the glial cells start searching for any neurons not being used and kill them. They also check every dendrite to see if it is being used and prune away all unused dendrites like trimming a tree. Micro glia move through the brain, searching for debris from broken off dendrites and dead neurons. They also prune away unused dendrites and help neurons make connections (Zimmer 2009). One astrocyte glia cell can wrap around more than a million synapses.

In this way, glial cells have a great influence on the brain. Radial glial cells also seem to be responsible for the creation of new neurons in adult brains. They then send out signals asking other glial cells where new neurons are needed and receive back an answer. They then herd the new neurons to that location and place the neurons where they are needed. To do this, they sometimes travel several inches through the brain. When they are all finished, they turn into astrocytes and hold the neural cell in place (Zimmer 2009). Some scientists believe that glial cells do analog computing by encoding information using calcium waves. Andrew Koob (2009) suggests that conversations among astrocytes using calcium waves may be responsible for our creativity and imagination (Zimmer 2009). It has also been learned that a certain protein can trigger glial cells into attacking and killing neurons. New discoveries about glial cells are being made every day. If, like me, you also have an interest in glial cells, simply search the Internet for glial cells and the present year. The biggest problem with the Internet is that most information is from the past and is obsolete. So, I always type in the year along with what I search for in order to learn about discoveries made this year.

It is hard to believe that chemicals moving through neurons and glial cells are all there is. Memories are nothing more than chemicals traveling from one neuron to another. The dendrite connections achieve memory (Rosenzweig 1984, 1996) and the breaking off of dendrites, or the pruning of dendrites by glial cells, is responsible for memory loss (Zimmer 2009). Relearning or new experience generates new dendrites and connections (Kleim et al. 1997).

The great thing about the brain is that if our brain needs

more neurons, it generates new neurons—a process called neurogenesis (Gage 2003; Mohapel, Leanza, and Lindvall 2010; Prickaerts et al. 2004; Wentz, Magavi, and Sanjay 2009; Camern, and Mckay 1999; Van Praag, Zhao, and Gage 2004). If neurons are not used and are needed for something else, then they are used for something else (Ruifang and Daning 2005). For example, when people become blind, the neurons normally used for sight are then rerouted by the glial cells to be used for touch and hearing (Amedi et al. 2005; Doyon and Benali 2005). If neurons are not used, and are not needed for something else, then they are eliminated by the glial cells (Zimmer 2009). In this way, our brain is always exactly what we need—that is, until our brain encounters some kind of disease or toxin. When free of disease, alcohol, nicotine, caffeine, drugs, toxins, radiation, etc., our brain is exactly what we need (Gage 2003; Mohapel et al. 2010; Prickaerts et al. 2004).

Students often ask if it is true that we only use 5 percent of our brains. That is ridiculous; neurons not used are eliminated (Zimmer 2009). What that actually means is that we are not living up to our potential. We can all study and learn far more than we know now. Most people are wasting their lives doing nothing when they could be doing so much. There is nothing better for our brains than education. Education is a lifelong process. Our brains change in response to our experiences and learning (Kempermann, Kuhn, and Gage 1997). This is called neural plasticity and it is a feedback loop. Learning creates changes in the brain which facilitates more learning which creates more changes in the brain which facilitates more learning and so on (Morris and Maisto 2010). In addition to that, neurogenesis is taking place in most people.

I say most because good nutrition, physical exercise (Van Praag et al. 2005), environmental complexity (Kempermann, Kuhn, and Gage 1997), and active learning must be present for neurogenesis to take place. Also, no alcohol, nicotine, caffeine, drugs, toxins, or radiation may be present (Monje et al. 2002; Noonan et al. 2010). Stress (Gould et al. 1997; Thomas and Peterson 2010; Wentz et al. 2009), and sleep deprivation (Guzman-Marin et al. 2005; Wentz et al. 2009; Mirescu and Gould 2006) will also decrease neurogenesis (Patoine, n.d.; Gage 2003; Wentz et al. 2009).

Adult neurogenesis can also be increased by a number of stimuli, including an enriched environment (Kempermann et al. 1997; Wentz et al.2009), exercise (Lafenetre et al. 2010; Lou et al. 2008), antidepressants (Malberg et al. 2000; Thomas and Peterson 2010; Duman, Nakagawa, and Malberg 2001; Santarelli et al. 2003; Wentz et al. 2009; Thomas and Peterson 2010), corticosteroids (Camern and McKay 1999; Wentz et al. 2009) pheromone exposure (Mak et al. 2007; Wentz et al. 2009) chronic high doses of cannabinoids, and chronic high doses of caffeine (Wentz et al. 2009; Perkins 2010; Jiang et al. 2005; Han et al. 2007). Even the removal of adrenal glands will increase adult neurogenesis (Wong 2006).

Caffeine has been found to be dosage dependent. Low and medium doses of caffeine decreases neurogenesis in mice, whereas extremely high doses of caffeine increase neurogenesis (Wentz et al. 2009). These extremely high doses of caffeine in human terms are equivalent to more than fifteen cups of coffee every day, day after day. Consumption of less than that amount significantly decreases neurogenesis (Wentz et al. 2009).

When I first learned this I thought that people consuming a lot of coffee with extreme amounts of caffeine may be doing the right thing. However, further studies of caffeine show that neurons created while consuming extremely high doses of caffeine die within about thirty days following neurogenesis (Wentz et al. 2009), which is about the same time most neurons are first being used by the brain. Therefore, all nerve cells created by consuming extremely high doses of caffeine die before they are used (Wentz et al. 2009; Han et al. 2007). Similar to this, high levels of estrogen increase neurogenesis of neurons, and those neurons also die before being used. This may also be true of nerve cells created by chronic high doses of cannabinoids. The brain may be responding to the destruction of brain cells by increasing neurogenesis and then the new neurons die because they are not needed or being used. If this is true, then the brain is giving us exactly what we need at all times without us trying to increase neurogenesis.

However, it is true that the average brain is shrinking with age. Could this be due to consumption of caffeine, alcohol, nicotine, and other drugs? In any case, I believe it is best to eliminate all drugs, including caffeine, and focus attention on good nutrition, physical exercise, and environmental complexity (Kempermann et al.1997, Wentz et al. 2009) and engage in active learning to increase neurogenesis. I consider continual education to be the most important.

Neurogenesis is a very slow process that occurs in multiple areas of the adult brain. It takes about one month for neural stem cells to be created, migrate to where they are needed, form dendrites and axons, mature into active neurons, and connect to other neurons. At first, the new neurons are very sensitive and experience a period of hyperactivity. Eventually, they are the same as all the other neurons (Patoine, n.d.; Gage 2003).

However, many people spend a lot of their time and money trying to damage their own brain. In our sick society, "dumbing down" is very popular. Intelligent people think about how things are and become depressed by telling themselves depressing messages. They could change these messages and end their depression. However, most people do not know how to do that. Instead, they turn to drugs that are very similar in chemical structure to the neurotransmitters in the neurons in their brain. These drugs fool the neurons into believing they are neurotransmitters, which slows down the speed of the nerve impulses which slows down their thinking, making them stupid. Stupid people are not depressed or bored. It is surprising what some people will do when they are depressed or bored. Some even go so far as spraying paint into a rag while smelling the rag. This is called huffing. What do you think that does to brain cells? However, most people turn to alcohol, nicotine, caffeine, and other drugs, which may be even worse for their brain. Everyone knows that alcohol destroys brain cells, but what about the most commonly used drug, caffeine?

Caffeine ($C_8H_{10}N_4O_2$) is a bitter alkaloid discovered by the German chemist Friedrich Ferdinand Runge in 1819. He named it Kaffein after the German word for coffee, Kaffee. The English changed the German word Kaffein into the English word caffeine.

Caffeine is both a pesticide and an herbicide. Coffee plants evolved containing caffeine for survival. Most insects die when they eat coffee plants because of caffeine. Most plants die within ten inches of coffee plants because the caffeine in the roots of the coffee plant kills all the plants around it, improving survival. Ninety percent of all Americans consume this pesticide and herbicide daily by choice. Caffeine causes difficulty falling asleep (Chait 1992), sleep disturbances, sleep deprivation (Guzman-Marin et al. 2005), increased anxiety (Clementz and Dailey 1988; Chait 1992), stress (Guzman-Marin et al. 2005), panic attacks (Clementz and Dailey 1988), depression (Guzman-Marin et al. 2005), and vasoconstrictive effects that can cause many problems, including changes in the brain (Palmer, Willhoite & Gage 2000).

I think of myself as being the sum total of all my memory. If memory is only the movement of chemicals, then I am only the movement of chemicals. This movement of chemicals never stops. I cannot stop this chemical movement, therefore I cannot stop thinking. Chemical movement and thinking continues during sleep and <u>what is experienced during sleep is called dreaming</u> (Atwell 1980). Even when a person is pronounced dead, this chemical movement continues for many hours and possibly for days (Stephey 2010). This is similar to the way that hair continues to grow after a person is pronounced dead.

A person is usually pronounced dead when the heart stops or the EEG flatlines. Neither of these indicates that chemical action has stopped in the brain. The heart stopping only indicates that blood has stopped flowing. It does not indicate that the person has stopped thinking. Chemical activity continues in the brain. Brains have been removed from guinea pigs, dogs, and monkeys. When supplied with oxygen and glucose, these brains have been kept alive for days after removal (Knowledge Magazine 2010).

Most people commonly perceive death as taking place in a moment. The heart stops and you're dead. However, today's technology is so improved that we can bring people back to life. In fact, drugs are now being developed that slow down brain-cell injury and death.

Dr. Sam Parnia, an expert on the scientific study of death, is interviewing 1,500 survivors of cardiac arrest. About 20 percent of these people have reported experiencing consciousness during death. Is this an illusion or is it real (Stephey 2010)?

When the heart stops, blood stops flowing. After five or ten minutes the neurons go into a kind of frenzy. After the frenzy stops, neurons start to change and slow down. However, chemical activity *does* continue for about two days until the body actually decomposes (Stephey 2010).

Death does not take place in a moment. Death may start when the heart stops, but the process of dying lasts for about two days. Chemicals continue to move in the brain for up to two days after the heart stops pumping blood. Chemical movement in the brain is what takes place during dreaming. Could it be that when people are in the process of dying, they are actually dreaming until the dream simply fades away as the chemicals slow down and eventually stop moving as the body decomposes (Stephey 2010)?

People continue to argue about when life starts, but few consider life to continue after the heart stops. Although they cannot talk to us, they do continue to hear us and they continue to think and dream for up to two days after the heart stops. Just think about the chicken running around after its head is cut off.

I feel much better knowing that when my heart stops, I will start dreaming and eventually my dream will simply fade away.

2
The Physiology of Sleep and Dreaming

The human brain releases a constant flow of electrical energy, which can be recorded and observed using an electroencephalograph (EEG). By placing electrodes, or small metal discs, on the scalp, this electrical energy is measured in millionths of a volt then amplified and recorded by the EEG by scratching a series of wavy lines, indicating brain-wave frequencies, onto a slowly moving paper (Foulkes 1962,1966, 1974).

These brain waves have been categorized into four frequencies:
- Beta waves at 14 to 30 cycles per second are associated with alertness, physical activity, excitement, fear, tension, and anxiety.
- Alpha waves at 8 to 13 cycles per second are associated with passive awareness, relaxation and general composure.
- Theta waves at 4 to 7 cycles per second are

associated with deep tranquility, euphoria, and very deep relaxation.
- Delta waves at 0.5 to 3.5 cycles per second are associated with deep sleep.

When desired, the EEG can also record muscle movements, sweating, and erections.

The EEG has been connected to many sleeping persons to record what takes place during sleep. These recordings show that mental activity does not cease at any time during sleep and some researchers have described cycles or stages of brain wave activity lasting approximately ninety minutes (Foulkes 1966).

On the following page is a composite drawing of the sleep cycle. It must be emphasized that this is an idealized picture of the average person's average night's sleep. There are also some variances, which I will discuss later.

To clarify understanding, this cycle has been divided into four stages according to the number of cycles per second of brain wave activity. Stage 1 has the most brain wave activity and stage 4 the least.

Stage 1 is also associated with Rapid Eye Movements (REM). During REM, both eyes generally move together. The eyes also move a little bit during stages 2, 3, and 4, but this is referred to as Non-Rapid Eye Movement (NREM).

According to J. A. Horne (1976), NREM sleep is more important for humans than REM sleep for the following reasons:
1. The importance of NREM sleep is apparent simply because of the need for NREM sleep to be fulfilled first, in that the first half of sleep is predominately NREM and the last half is predominately REM—that

is, assuming that the bodily need with the highest priority is fulfilled first.
2. Naturally short sleepers and naturally long sleepers spend approximately the same amount of time in NREM sleep.
3. The percentage of NREM sleep is much greater for people on enforced limited sleep regimes than for normal sleepers.
4. Evidence suggests the possible dispensability of REM sleep.
5. REM deprivation has no serious detrimental effects in humans.
6. Subjects can be deprived of REM sleep, but cannot be deprived of NREM sleep.
7. NREM is related to the prior length of wakefulness, while REM is not (Horne 1976). During Stage 1 (REM) the autonomic nervous system shows greater irregularities in pulse, respiration rates, and in blood pressure. Both male and female erections have been observed (Karacan, Rosenbloom, and Williams 1970). There is a higher rate of oxygen consumption in the brain, and the brain stem and brain become intensely active with a rise in temperature. Most muscles are flaccid, although twitching is sometimes observed. Major body movements, such as turning over in bed, increase immediately prior to and just after stage 1 (REM). During stage 1 (REM) it is harder to be aroused by a stimulus, such as a noise or touch, than during stage 4 (NREM). Stage 1 (REM) is a state of heightened activity equivalent to an equal period of jogging (Cartwright 1977).

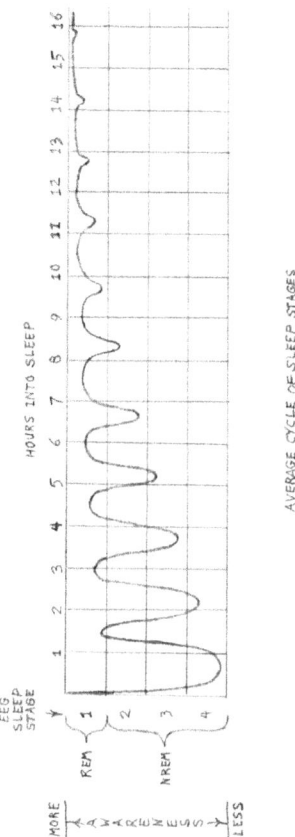

Studies of stage 1 (REM) suggest that it contributes to divergent thinking and adaptation to new situations (Glaubman et al. 1978). Other studies suggest it contributes to information processing (Zimmerman, Stoyva, and Reite 1978; Hobson 1969; Peterfreund and Schwartz 1971).

Of the thousands tested so far, no person has been tested who does not show a similar average cycle. Persons suffering from narcolepsy, a disease characterized by an uncontrollable urge for sleep, are an exception in that stage 1 (REM) occurs at their sleep onset. Their cycle is identical in all other ways. Stage 2 (NREM) occurs at the onset of sleep for all other persons (Foulkes 1966; Vogel 1960; Rechtschaffen et al. 1963). Stage 2 (NREM) also occurs at the onset of daytime naps (Rechtschaffen and Verdone 1964; Maron, Rechtschaffen, and Wolpert 1964).

Michel Jouvet (2001) has demonstrated that destruction of the nucleus reticularis pontis caudalis, a portion of the pons, abolishes stage 1 (REM) in cats. He also showed that brief stimulation of the same structure during NREM sleep produces Stage 1 (REM), which lasts ten to fifteen minutes. There is also a rather unique pattern of electrical activity (4 to 7 cps spikes) in the pons during REM sleep (Foulkes 1966).

This seems to indicate that the sleep cycle is dependent on electrical activity or some biological rhythm of the pons. This cycle also seems to be taking place during wakefulness.

Early sleep and dream researchers mistakenly jumped to two conclusions (Dement and Kleitman 1957). First, the movements of the eyes during stage 1 (REM) indicated that the eyes were moving in unison to observe dreaming. During NREM, eyes did not move in unison due to lack of dreams to observe (Koulack 1972). Second, they assumed that dreaming only took place during REM and that NREM was altogether devoid of psychological experience. Unfortunately, these two conclusions were printed in many books, and this created two more myths. Research has shown both of these to be incorrect. Eye movements during stage 1 (REM) are in no way connected with dream content (Foulkes 1966; Koulack 1972;

Krippner, Cavallo, and Keenan 1972). Eyes move in unison during stage 1 (REM) due only to physiology, and dreaming just also happens to be taking place. Dreaming does take place during NREM (Foulkes 1966,) although the quality of dreaming during REM may be better than during NREM due to increased brain activity, which increases awareness. However, Dement and Kleitman found that "mental content of a distinctive quality can be reliably elicited from NREM sleep" (Foulkes 1966).

Those who insist that dreaming only takes place during stage 1 (REM) quote Dement and Kleitman (1957). That was the first study of this kind and used the most strict "detailed" dream description for their criterion of recall. Failure of dream recall from NREM awakenings to meet this criterion did not mean that dreaming did not take place during NREM, only that it did not meet their strict definition of what a dream is. Even with a strict definition of what a dream is, they still found dreams meeting that definition with 7 percent NREM recall.

The first independent confirmation found 53 percent NREM recall compared with the 7 percent NREM recall of Dement and Kleitma (1957). Even with 53 percent, the authors still attributed all NREM recall to the memory of previous stage 1 (REM) dreams as Dement and Kleitman (1957) had done (Foulkes 1966).

Kamiya (1962) did an extensive study with 906 awakenings and found 86 percent NREM recall. Although his criterion was not as strict as Dement and Kleitman's (1957) study, there was still 28 percent NREM recall when applying their very strict criterion.

What was important about Kamiya's (1962) work was that he also proved that NREM recall was not memory from previous REM dreams. He did this by making NREM awakenings before any REM periods had occurred. The first REM period occurs approximately ninety minutes after sleep onset. In this way, he proved that dreaming does take place during NREM as well as during REM periods (Kamiya 1962).

David Foulkes (1966) asked subjects what they were experiencing and taped their responses, rather than asking them about their "dreams." He did this because he believed that in the previous studies in which subjects were asked about their "dreams," the subjects were making the decision as to what a dream was, and whether or not what they had experienced met that definition.

When using a criterion similar to that of Kamiya's (1962,) Foulkes (1966) found 74 percent NREM recall with 136 NREM awakenings and 87 percent REM recall with 108 REM awakenings. NREM stages 2, 3, and 4 all ranged within 4 percent of the 74 percent average. These same percentages of dream recall were identical when awakenings were made before stage 1 (REM) had occurred. This proved that dream recall during NREM is not remembered from REM. When "claims" of mental content were added to the specific mental content, there was 87 percent NREM recall and 92 percent REM recall with some mental activity. Dreaming does take place during all stages of sleep (Foulkes 1966).

Niedermeyer and Lentz (1976) did an extensive study with 140 subjects and found that 16 percent of the subjects recalled dreams during NREM sleep.

A study of nightmares by Charles Fisher, Joseph Byrne,

and Adele Edwards (1968) found that 73 percent of thirty-four observed nightmares occurred in the first NREM period.
A study of NREM dreaming by R. L. Van de Castle and Peter Hauri (1970) concluded that: "psychophysiological parallelism between autonomic measures and quality of mentation may exist throughout the whole range of sleep."

Edwin Kahn, Charles Fisher, Adele Edwards, and David Davis (1973) studied night terrors (stage 4 NREM); 275 arousals during night terrors showed a 58 percent dream recall. Arthur Arkin, John Antrobus, Max Toth, Julia Baker, and Frances Jackler (1972) studied sleep utterance and NREM dreaming. They concluded that many NREM sleep utterances arise out of ongoing NREM dreaming and "provide valid indices of NREM mental content because the two types of reports are indistinguishable." The content and quantity of NREM dream recall associated with sleep utterance is essentially similar to NREM dream recall without utterance. However, subjects are much more likely to report dream recall when they were actively talking in the dream when awakened during or immediately following sleep utterance. Subjects could remember what words they said in the dream, but did not know they had said the words out loud. The authors compared this to people talking to themselves aloud without knowing they could be heard (Arkin et al.1972).

I believe that earlier experimenters found low NREM recall percentages due to the following:
1. Unknown differences and variability in remembering by subjects employed.

2. Small numbers of subjects were employed. Only nine subjects were employed in Dement and Kleitman's study and only five contributed the bulk of the data (Foulkes 1966; Dement and Kleitman 1957).
3. Differences in interview technique.
4. Differences in criterion and definitions of what a dream is.
5. The experimenter's expectations as to what the results would show.
6. Subjects wanting to please experimenters with what they guessed were desired.
7. Variations in experiment environment.
8. Discounting NREM recall to be remembered from previous REM without investigation.
9. Variability in recall may be greater for NREM than for REM.

Even though dreaming takes place during all stages of sleep, there is a qualitative difference between REM and NREM, which may be due to brain wave activity, which increases awareness.

NREM dreaming and REM dreaming are not independent of each other. There seems to be a continuation of dream theme content. NREM continues the theme of the preceding REM and REM continues the theme of the preceding NREM.

Rechtschaffen, Vogel, and Shaikun (1963) systematically investigated the interrelatedness of REM and NREM dreaming. Subjects were awakened several times during a single night while in different stages of sleep and their experiences were recorded. They found a close relationship between REM and NREM. Discrete elements and themes in NREM sometimes repeat, and sometimes anticipate, the content of other NREM and REM periods of the same night. They concluded that dreams are not psychologically isolated productions, but are the most vivid and memorable part of mental activity during sleep.

NREM dreams are generally less emotional, less elaborate, less dramatic, and have fewer characters. NREM dreams are more likely to correspond to recent events or daily routines, such as school or work, and are more likely to "make sense" to the dreamer (Foulkes 1966).

Research has shown that there are individual differences in the percentage of stage 1 REM sleep (Rechtscchaffen and Verdone 1964; Antrobus, Dement, and Fisher 1964). Every person generally has the same percentage of stage 1 REM sleep night after night that is fairly constant. There are individual differences in the percentages, but those differences are of a very slight magnitude. One twenty-subject study found a mean of 24.2 percent REM, a standard deviation of 3.4 percent, and a range of 19.4 percent to 33.3 percent (Rechtscchaffen and Verdone 1964). Another study found that actively ill schizophrenics had 19.6 percent (Feinberg et al. 1964).

I want to emphasize that all of these percentages are only for the first seven hours of sleep. The longer the sleep period, the higher the percentage of stage 1 REM time. I am only trying to show here that personality factors do relate to the percentage of stage 1 REM time sleep. However, it is within a very small range.

One study suggests that there are two separate requirements for sleep with a relatively constant requirement for stages 2, 3, and 4. The requirement for stage 1 may be related to the individual's personality and/or lifestyle (Hartmann et al. 1971).

Monroe (1965) investigated self-described "good" and "poor" sleepers. He found a big difference in Minnesota Multiphasic Personality Inventory (MMPI) profiles between the two groups. The self-described "poor" sleepers averaged higher psychopathological scores on twelve out of thirteen scales. The Cornell Medical Index also revealed more psychosomatic complaints and emotional disturbance for the "poor" sleepers.

"Poor" sleepers were found to have significantly less stage 1 REM sleep. They had the same number of stage 1 REM periods, but the periods were shorter in length. This was partly attributed to numerous spontaneous awakenings during stage 1. "Poor" sleepers had higher rectal temperatures, faster heart rate, increased pulse volume, more frequent phasic vasoconstrictions, and more body mobility during sleep than "good" sleepers.

Self-described "good" and "poor" sleepers are generally viewed as "healthy" and "neurotic" personalities. However, it has not yet been determined which of the associated variables of physiological arousal, neuroticism, and amount of stage 1 REM sleep might be cause and which effect (Foulkes 1966).

There are also differences in percentages of stage 1 REM time due to age. Newborn infants spend about 50 percent of sleep in stage 1 REM; at age two about 40 percent; at age five about 30 percent; adults about 25 percent; and age sixty about 15 percent. Human fetuses are estimated to spend about 98 percent of sleep in stage 1 REM (Cartwright 1977; Hartmann

1967; Jones 1970; Regush and Regush 1977). Senile people have very little stage 1 REM sleep. There is speculation that senility may someday be abolished by the administration of drugs to increase stage 1 REM time.

A study by Hume and Mills (1977) concluded that the amount of NREM sleep is dependent on the duration of prior wakefulness. When a person experiences a loss of sleep, either an entire night or deprivation of certain stages in a sleep laboratory, the sleep pattern will shift to compensate for the loss (Cartwright 1977; Faraday 1973; Tart 1972). For example, if a person stays awake twenty-four hours or longer before sleeping, there will be a prolonged period of stages 3 and 4 at sleep onset followed by a 30 percent increase in the percentage of stage 1 REM time.

John S. Antrobus and associates have demonstrated that REM also occurs during daydreaming and visual imagery (Antrobus, Antrobus, and Singer 1964).

David Cohen (1973, 1977) studied right and left hemisphere dominance of REM periods. He found a consistent increase in left hemisphere control/dominance across the REM periods during the night. This relation was also attenuated for left-handed subjects. The author's hypothesis is that "efficient sleep" can be thought of as "a process by which the individual is gradually prepared to resume, upon awakening, the normal, dominant hemisphere-mediated functioning that presumably characterizes the waking state."

Judith Brown and Rosalind Cartwright (1978) did an extensive study of dreaming by teaching subjects to signal when they were dreaming. They concluded that subjects could more accurately judge when they were dreaming than could the experimenters. The reason for this is that experimenters cannot determine if subjects are dreaming during NREM by watching an EEG. REM and NREM are no longer considered to be an objective indicator of dreaming. They also concluded that frequency of NREM dreaming signals varied with pre-sleep mood.

Now, are all these dream studies using the EEG of any value? Researchers now believe the EEG is of no value or very little value at most when studying dreaming (Giora and Elam 1974; Fedio et al. 1961). There are even some who doubt whether EEG activity in waking and in sleep depicts the same mental functions. Johnson (1970) believes that brain waves in waking and sleep do not come from the same "generator."

Evarts (1961) studied EEG activity and neurons in both waking and sleep in cats. He found that different sets of neurons are active during waking and sleep, even though the EEG activity is similar (Evarts 1961; Giora and Elam 1974). Although this study has not been made on humans, Johnson suggests that the results may be the same (Giora and Elam, 1974; Johnson 1970). If so, there may be more than one source for similar brain waves. Similar EEG tracings may have different meanings.

Fedio and his associates did a study of schizophrenics and concluded the "EEG alone does not reliably identify states of consciousness" (Fedio 1974). They also state "We have enough evidence to substantiate the view that "dreams" occur in all hours of sleep, during both REM and NREM sleep" (Giora and Elam 1974).

Obviously, cognition never ceases while we are alive. Dreaming is ongoing throughout sleep. I agree with Foulkes that "no point of absolute dream onset exists . . . There is no point in the sleep cycle at which consciousness suddenly appears. It seems to be there all along" (Giora and Elam 1974; Foulkes 1964; Foulkes and Vogel 1965; Hobson, Goldfrank, and Snyder 1965; Zimmerman 1967).

It is obvious to me that the EEG cannot be used to determine whether or not a person is dreaming because dreaming is continuous throughout sleep. I even doubt whether or not the EEG can show the vividness of dreaming, in that "night terrors" take place during stage 4 NREM. As far as the sleep cycle is concerned, it is only an average. There are many NREM periods during REM and many REM periods during NREM. The EEG is too vague an instrument with which to study dreaming and more sophisticated equipment must be invented and connected to computers for interpretation.

3
Remembering Dreams

The **"I-never-dream" notion** is one of the prominent myths. I am amazed at how many people tell me that they never dream. Every person dreams every time they sleep, even during daytime naps. Dreaming is continuous throughout sleep (Garfield 1974).

Taking this one step further, I don't believe I know how to stop thinking. I like believing that I am continually aware (thinking, feeling, and sensing), awake and asleep. Any awareness during sleep is what I call dreaming.

People dream most of the time—if not all of the time they are asleep—every time they sleep. Most of their many dreams are not remembered; only a few dreams are remembered. The difference is in their remembering instead of whether they dream or not. This is summarized from the first chapter.

Although I disagree with Levenson (1974) and Lowy (1942) as to what the purpose of the dream is, I do agree that a dream need not be remembered to have served its purpose. I am not concerned that there is something wrong when I do not remember dreams. I only feel that I am missing out on many beautiful and exciting experiences. This does not mean that I did not have the experience. I experience every dream fully at the time of the dream, whether I remember it or not. What I miss out on is remembering the experience.

In the dream groups I lead, I have noticed that people who say they never dream refer to dreams as "nightmares" far more than those who say they dream. These "nondreamers" usually ask questions such as, "Why would anyone want to remember nightmares?" or "If a person remembered all their dreams, wouldn't they be depressed all the time?" and "But what if a person has nightmares?"

There are many factors that determine whether or not I remember a dream. There is far more to remembering dreams than just wanting to. However, repression is not responsible for not remembering dreams (Cohen 1973; Cohen and Wolfe 1973). I consider my desire to remember and my interest in dreams to be the most important factor in remembering my dreams. I remember far more dreams since I started studying dreams and writing this book.

Several people who have attended my dream groups have told me that their ability to remember dreams increased after they started therapy. My guess is that their therapist showed an interest in their dreams and that either their wanting to please their therapist or their learning that dreams are important enabled them to remember. This is what Dr. Ernest Schachtel (1959) called "sensitized to awareness" (Diamond 1963).

Persons claiming that they never dream often turn into vivid recallers after attending dream groups. This may be due to their learning how valuable dreams can be, a desire to know themselves better, or just a simple curiosity. Since dreaming is basically a continuation of waking, thinking about dreaming while awake will carry over into sleep and create an interest in remembering dreams (Faraday 1974; McLeester 1976).

Some people actually train themselves to wake up when they become aware of experiencing a vivid dream so that they can write it down (Cayce 1962).

I am often aware that I am dreaming and don't wake up. In fact, I would rather continue dreaming. Every time I do wake up, I am dreaming. In fact, every time people awaken naturally without an outside stimulus, they awaken from stage 1 REM sleep. Awakening from NREM can only be initiated by an outside source. Those few persons who suffer from "night terrors" are an exception.

There have been studies that have subjects signal when they are aware that they are dreaming, although I believe that the subjects were actually trained to signal when they were experiencing REM sleep, instead of when they were experiencing dreaming. At that time, researchers were still under the misconception that dreaming only took place during stage 1 REM.

For example, Judith Antrobus, John Antrobus, and Charles Fisher (1965) asked four subjects to close a micro switch taped to one hand whenever they were aware of dreaming. All four subjects signaled more often during stage 1 REM than during NREM. Salamy replicated this study in 1970 and increased the signaling by adding a "punishment" for not signaling during any stage 1 REM period (Cartwright 1977).

However, looking past the subjects being trained to signal during REM instead of during dreaming, these two studies show that subjects are aware and able to take action during sleep.

I consider pre-sleep intention to be very important in remembering dreams and I plan to remember at least one dream every time I sleep. In fact, I expect to remember my dreams and I am surprised when I don't. On those occasions when I wake up not remembering a dream, my solution is simply to go back to sleep. This is almost always successful. However, I sometimes sleep a third time.

When I started studying dreams, I only remembered about one dream a week and thought there was something wrong with me, since I didn't dream more often than once a week. So, several times a day and every time I went to bed, I thought phrases like "I want to dream tonight," "I am going to dream tonight," and "I will dream tonight," while falling asleep. This increased the number of dreams I remembered. Naturally, when I learned that I dream several dreams every time I sleep, I changed the phrase to "I will remember a dream," and "I will remember my dreams." Now that my dreams are easy to remember, I no longer do this.

This is similar to what is done with hypnosis. A friend who said she did not dream told me that she remembered a dream after attending a hypnosis group and receiving a suggestion to remember her dreams.

Many dream experts say that a sudden awakening normally results in more dream recall than a gradual awakening (Diamond 1963; Faraday 1973). This has given rise to a new myth due to misunderstanding rather than misinformation. Readers take this to mean that when they awaken suddenly by an alarm clock or telephone ringing they have a better chance of remembering a dream than if they slowly wake up spontaneously on their own. I find just the opposite to be true, in my own experience.

When researchers talk about sudden and gradual awakenings, they are referring to sudden and gradual awakenings by external stimuli in a sleep laboratory, such as bells and touch. They are not referring to spontaneous awakenings.

When I wake up to the sound of an alarm, I usually get out of bed with the intention of shaving and getting dressed to drive to work. I focus my attention on what I have to do. This change in my attention causes me to forget my dreams. David Cohen (1974) found that normal behavior like this seems largely responsible for the forgetting of dreams.

When awakening by an alarm, other than in a sleep laboratory, there is a good chance of awakening during an NREM period. All spontaneous awakenings occur from REM periods, allowing a better chance to remember due to the increased brain wave activity.

The easiest way for me to remember my dreams is to sleep as long as possible and awaken slowly and spontaneously with nothing to do but sleep and dream. Notice how much easier it is to remember dreams on weekends than on workdays. Any distraction like the telephone ringing wipes out my dream memory because I divert my thinking away from the dream to the telephone. Hermann Rorschach, the inventor of the famous "inkblot" personality projection test, believed dreams were sensory experiences derived from the movements of muscles. He advised people not to open their eyes and to lie perfectly still because any quick motor movements, like getting out of bed, would disrupt memory. I do not believe dreams are sensory experiences derived from the movements of muscles. I do advise lying in bed as long as possible to increase memory for the reasons I have already mentioned.

When I first started reading dream books, I got very excited about personality types. Some of this excitement was due to my being classified as a recaller and I liked what was said about recallers. Most books classify persons into two categories, recallers (recalling two dreams or more a month) and nonrecallers (recalling less than two dreams a month).

Nonrecallers are generally considered to be extroverts, outer-oriented, repressors, handle problems by denying them, defensive, over-controlled, confident, inhibited, conformist, avoid or deny unpleasant experiences, and hard to wake up.

Recallers are generally considered to be introverted, inner-oriented, more willing to admit emotional disturbances such as anxiety and insecurity, overtly anxious about life, more self-aware, easy to wake up, more capable of visual imagery outside of dreams, and are able to use visual imagery more often and effectively. One study even concluded that firstborns recall fewer dreams than laterborn (Ward et al. 1973).

I now consider these to only be guesses. I don't believe enough is known at the present time to justify such generalizations. My guess is that what is different about recallers and nonrecallers may be a secondary characteristic, such as lifestyle. This hypothesis has been supported by the work of David Cohen. He compared dream recall frequency for monozygotic and dizygotic twins, non-twin siblings, and friends. Findings indicated dream recall frequency is partially determined by lifestyles rather than genetic similarity (Cohen 1973).

I live a very unique lifestyle with no time schedule; I stay awake when I can't sleep and sleep when I can't stay awake. I often stay awake as long as forty-eight hours and sleep as long as sixteen hours. This allows me a greater awareness of dreaming while dreaming, and a spontaneous awakening from REM, with nothing scheduled to do after awakening to distract me from remembering my dreams. Plus, I have an added feature of having someone to share my dreams with when I awake. Leading dream groups, reading dream books, sharing dreams with friends, writing this book, and using my dreams for self-therapy all aid in my remembering dreams. A study by Henry Reed (1973) also concluded that discussing dreams with others is helpful in increasing dream recall.

Goodenough and Shapiro (1959) found one important difference between those who claimed they were nondreamers and dreamers. The nondreamers seemed to mislabel their dream experiences. When they were awakened during sleep, they would report that they were "awake and thinking" or "asleep and thinking" (Goodenough 1959). This indicates that people who claim to be nondreamers may have a different definition of what dreaming actually is.

Most of my dreams are very similar to my everyday life. Also, a study by Marion Hendricks (1975) concluded that people tend to dream about content with which their waking life is occupied. Also, sex role orientation rather than biological gender plays a fundamental role in determining dream content (Cohen 1973). However, remembering this similarity of dreams and waking life is like remembering the similarity of yesterday and the day before. When remembering what I did on each day, I remember what was different, unusual, exciting, and I forget those things that were the same, usual, and boring. To better illustrate this, remember what you were thinking yesterday afternoon and compare it with your thinking of the afternoon the day before.

"Exciting and emotional dreams," sometimes referred to as "nightmares," are far easier to remember than "pleasant" dreams (Cohen 1974). I know this is true for me even though I don't remember having a "nightmare"; I like believing that I no longer have them. I like believing that my working with my dreams, acting them out, accepting them as part of me, creating an awareness that I am dreaming while dreaming, accepting that I create every one of my dreams exactly the way I want that dream, and becoming more creative and purposely creating my dreams, have all contributed to my no longer choosing to create "nightmares." Whether this is true or not, I don't know. I do know I now have more sex and far less fear in my dreams than ever before. Of course, this is also true for my waking life. I wonder which came first.

Alexander Randall (1978) conducted a study during a month-long residential conference on dreams. The content analysis of all the group members' dreams revealed that over the course of the month, dream images of violence declined while sexual imagery increased.

Weiner (1966) concluded after a literature review that any experience with intense emotions of any type is more likely to be remembered than nonemotional experiences (Francher and Strahan 1971; Weiner 1966).

This "nightmares-are-easier-to-remember" principle also applies to dreams that seem to be very important or full of psychological meaning or that make a lot of sense. This also applies to dreams interpreted to reveal "latent homosexuality," dreams believed to be a message from God or predicting the future, a recurring dream, or any other unique dream.

A man recently came to one of my groups with a dream he had been carrying around with him since childhood. He had been in psychoanalysis for the past six years without revealing this dream to his psychoanalyst. He said he was afraid that if he told him the dream, he would either make something bizarre out of it or it would "open up a can of worms." He came to my group to find out what I thought his dream meant. After being told to tell the dream in first person, present tense, he told the dream as follows:

I am in a public men's restroom with four toilets that are surrounded by the usual metal partitions. I am sitting on the toilet on the end to my right. There is a space of about one foot between the bottom of these partitions and the floor. I am wondering if there is anyone else sitting on another toilet. So, I am leaning over to see if I can see anyone. At the exact same time another person is doing the exact same thing on the toilet at the other end. Only the other person is wearing a mask so that I cannot see who they are. We are staring at each other and I am very frightened.

Each member of the group participated by becoming one part of his dream and together acted out the entire dream. Next, he was asked to change the dream in any way he wanted and the group acted out the new version. He experienced a lot of emotion, seemed very relieved, and said he now wanted to tell this dream to his psychoanalyst.

I had a pleasant reaction to hearing his dream. His believing it was capable of "opening up a can of worms" created the energy to hold on to it and carry it with him for years. My "can of worms" usually turns out to be a "bouquet of flowers" and the opening of each flower is a present to myself.

Not only is remembering dreams not encouraged in our culture, it is also discouraged. Dreaming is discounted as being one of the unexplained and ridiculous things people do. When I was a child, my parents often comforted me by saying: "It was only a dream. Just forget it and go back to sleep. I'll turn on the light so that you can see it's not real." And when I told them my dreams, they were met with laughter or boredom. Over time, this had a strong, discouraging effect on me. Even though I continued to remember my dreams, I stopped telling anyone about them.

Sharing dreams with others is very important. Even talking about not remembering dreams will be an important step toward remembering them. In other cultures, like the Senoi of Malaya, parents and children all share their dreams every morning at breakfast. The sharing of dreams, plus parents believing them important, encourages the remembering of dreams.

Quite often, people come to my groups and say they do not dream and I have them make up or create a dream for the group. I then work with this made-up dream in the same way as an actual dream. I can learn about myself by working with made-up dreams as well as with real dreams. This focuses attention on dreaming and sparks interest in remembering dreams.

Recallers (those who remember two or more dreams a month) are considered to have a greater capacity for visual imagery outside of dreams and use visual imagery more often and effectively (Hiscock and Cohen 1973). Possibly, if nonrecallers would increase their use of visual imagery outside of dreams, they might become recallers. This can also be done with guided fantasy, fantasy trips, and self-hypnosis.

Drugs may affect sleep the same way they affect nonsleep. Stimulants may decrease dream memory and dreaming. Alcohol and sleeping pills may be the worst enemies of dream memory and dreaming. Barbiturates even reduce the number of Rapid Eye Movements.

I have learned a few ways to facilitate my remembering dreams. The first method I learned was to set my alarm to ring several times during the night. I experimented with different time periods and found that they all worked. I stopped using this method when I found out that anytime I awaken naturally I awaken from REM. I also sleep as long as possible each time I sleep, knowing that awareness increases the longer I sleep. The most effective way is to stay awake as long as possible (thirty-six hours, forty-eight hours, or longer) and then sleep as long as possible with nothing to do all day, to assure memory. Staying awake twenty-four hours or more will increase REM during the next sleep by at least 30 percent, which I believe increases awareness of dreaming and recall. David Cohen (1972) has demonstrated that total sleep time is a significant predictor variable for dream recall.

When all this fails and I wake up not remembering any dreams, the solution is simple. I just go back to sleep and dream again. In my opinion, not remembering a dream is the best reason for staying in bed and going back to sleep.

4
The Evolution of Dream Theory

I wonder when our ancestors first started dreaming. All mammals tested so far experience REM and are believed to dream. Even opossums, which are not mammals, experience as much REM as humans (Dement 1976).

I understand octopuses are far more intelligent than anyone believes. My guess is that octopuses dream. Fantasize with me for a moment. What would an octopus dream about? My guess would be that an octopus dreams about their interactions with other octopuses, predators trying to eat them, searching for food, etc. In other words, their dream life would be very similar to their waking life. I consider it rather ridiculous to imagine an octopus going to a professional octopus and discussing their dreams in order to find out what their dreams mean or the purpose of their dreams.

At what point in our evolution did dreaming first begin?

I do not know. I do believe that our ancestors experienced dreaming *before* evolving into mammals and I also believe that many non-mammals dream—possibly all animals dream, even insects. A dream is what the dreamer experiences while asleep. Using this definition, most life forms dream. Animal dreaming needs much further study. In any case, dreaming has been experienced for millions of years.

According to Tylor (1978), our ancestors were greatly confused about dreaming only a few thousand years ago. He assumed that our ancestors at one time had similar beliefs to those of the primitive cultures of today. He made a study of these primitive cultures and found that two things trouble them most. The first is the difference between a living person and a dead person. The second is what takes place during dreaming. They confuse dreaming with waking life. They are most confused by the appearance of dead relatives in their dreams. These primitive people concluded that there must be another person, an exact double, living inside every person. This other person is responsible for movement, because when this other person leaves, movement stops. This, they explain, is what is taking place during death, fainting, and sleep (Tylor 1978; Diamond 1963).

They had two theories as to what was taking place during sleep. The first was that this other person inside left the body and did things and had experiences and then came back to the body. Dreams were what were remembered of the out-of-the-body experiences. The second theory was that the other person from inside other people or dead people came to visit them while they slept (Tylor 1978; Diamond 1963). In addition, the Kiwai Papuans of British New Guinea also believe that if a sorcerer can catch their soul while out-of-the-body, they will never wake up.

According to Tylor (1978), dreams and this confusion and belief about dreaming by our ancestors created primitive religions and these primitive religions evolved into our present-day religions. Confusion about dreaming is responsible for the religious belief in a soul and life after death. These two beliefs are important concepts of every major religion today. Religion has been responsible for the killing of millions of people all over the world for thousands of years and the killing still continues today. If Tylor is correct, those people died simply because our ancestors did not understand their dreams (De Becker 1968).

Dreams also played a major role in the evolution of our present-day religions. The dreams of the New Testament seem absolutely essential to Christianity. True, the angel of the Lord appeared in them and guaranteed their supernatural truth. No one considered them to be anything else (De Becker 1968). For example, Matthew 1:20: "But while he thought on these things, behold, the angel of the Lord appeared unto him in a dream, saying, Joseph, thou son of David, fear not to take unto thee Mary thy wife: for that which is conceived in her is of the Holy Ghost." There are 217 references to dreams in the Talmud. Also, Buddhism, Hinduism, and Islam all rely heavily on dreams. Mohammad received his divine messages in dreams. Dreams are extremely important to the creation of all the world's religions.

The earliest known dream book belonged to the Egyptian Pharaoh Merikare of the Xth dynasty, about 2070 BC. He believed dreams to be intuitive forays into the future (O'Nell 1976; De Becker 1968).

Fragments of other Egyptian dream books, Carlsberg papyri XIII and XIV, as well as the Chester Beatty papyrus III, also survive from about 1800 BC, in which dreams were interpreted as either good or bad omens, opposite to what would be expected (De Becker 1968; O'Nell 1976). For example, one very common dream subject, which was interpreted to be a good omen, was that of eating human flesh. Their believing this to be a good omen may account for it being a very common dream in their culture and a very rare dream in ours.

By 600 BC the Assyrians believed that dreams were caused by afflictions, which could be relieved if the dream could be interpreted to reveal the source of the affliction (O'Nell 1976).

Ancient Hinduism suggested that the world was a dream of Brahma, meaning that this world we live in is only a dream of God. They were the first to interpret dream symbols, linking them to wakeful experience or future events (O'Nell 1976).

By the fourth century BC, the Chinese had the *I Ching* (*Book of Changes*), composed of hexagrams based on symbolic images, which were applied to dream imagery as well as to other mysterious patterns in the human experience. Important factors in assessing the meaning of a dream were: important events in the dreamer's life; the social situation; the psychological state; year, season and day of the dream; the part of the night in which the dream occurred; astrological factors; and the respective situation of the great forces of yin and yang (O'Nell 1976).

The Chinese Taoists used dreams for self-knowledge by classifying them according to cause. The cause of the dream revealed physical or mental changes, which, if understood, permitted the dreamer to cope better with personal problems through self-knowledge (O'Nell 1976).

Hippocrates, the founder of modern medicine, and later Aristotle, placed greater emphasis on the importance of dreams than did most of their contemporaries or those who came later, like Plato, who believed that all dreaming took place in the liver (Diamond 1963). They believed that illness could be diagnosed by dreams. Aristotle also argued against dreams being messages from God (Coxhead 1976; O'Nell 1976). He believed that during sleep we are capable of more refined observations of subtle bodily occurrences and we are less occupied with plans and principles of action and have more internal awareness than when awake (Fromm 1951).

In the second century, Artemidorus spent most of his life studying dreams. He wrote five books of *Oneirocritica*, which are a Hellenic model of the analytical approach. Two books were on how to interpret dreams, in which he insisted that in order to interpret a dream, as much information as possible must be obtained about the dreamer's character, mood, and life situation. The other three books consisted of long lists of dream interpretations divided into categories by subject (Coxhead 1976; Regush and Regush 1977). Of course, the major belief throughout the centuries, and erroneously believed by religious fanatics even now, is that dreams are either messages from God or visitations from demons. This was reflected in the Babylonian Talmud, with rules both for interpreting and avoiding dreams.

Mohammed believed dreams were conversations between man and Allah (O'Nell 1976). He gave instructions for what to do when you wake up from a dream that you do not like. 1. Spit three times on your left side. 2. Ask for shelter from Allah. 3. Turnover and go back to sleep.

The Roman belief that dreams were most important for divinatory and oracular purpose was challenged by Cicero. He asked why gods would communicate to men in such an unreliable manner instead of speaking directly to them (O'Nell 1976).

After the early medieval period, dreams came more and more into disrepute in the church, but maintained popular appeal. St. Augustine and St. Ambrose both prayed to be spared from dreaming. St. Thomas Aquinas, one of the greatest thinkers in Catholicism, believed in the divination of dreams (messages from both God and the devil foretelling future events), but even if they revealed truth, he thought dreams were sinful because divination always implicates the devil. This belief eventually linked dreams with witchcraft and dreams were sometimes the only evidence brought against a witch. Dreamers had come into league with the devil and were burned at the stake (O'Nell 1976).

There were many dream books produced in Europe after the Renaissance that were traceable to the work of Artemidorus. Unfortunately, most were mechanical and lacking the flexibility and understanding that Artemidorus developed. These books were dictionaries of dream symbols with meanings assigned. Dream symbol dictionaries, still being printed and sold in bookstores today, can be traced back to Artemidorus in the second century.

I personally make it a rule not to buy any dream book that contains a dictionary of any kind. Even a few pages in a dictionary style are enough to show that the book was either written hundreds of years ago and that the author is out of date and uninformed.

Dictionary and cookbook-style dream books only confuse readers into believing that each dream "symbol" has a specific meaning instead of being subjective projections of the dreamer.

5
Iroquoi

Jesuit Missionaries came from France to America from 1610 to 1791. They came to "save" the Native Americans by converting them to Catholicism. In addition, they lived with them to study their language, customs, and religion.

These Jesuit missionaries made an extensive study of the Iroquoi. The Iroquoi confederation was composed of six Native American tribes. The missionaries wrote about everything they did and learned in journals, which were shipped back to France. Those many journals were eventually compiled into several books. Those books were later translated into English and publish as *The Jesuit Relations and Allied Documents*, which were several volumes. I read all those volumes with amazement (Ragueneau 1959).

The Jesuit Missionaries kept records both on how many were "saved" and how many died from the diseases the missionaries brought with them. They once wiped out an entire village with smallpox. Some journals subtracted the number that died from the number "converted" to equal their success.

Often the number that died exceeded the number "saved" (Ragueneau 1959).

The Jesuits studied the religion of the Iroquoi and found that dreams were a major part of their religion. The Iroquoi believed that every dream must be acted out in real life exactly as dreamed (Ragueneau 1959). The Jesuit journals were filled with dreams the Iroquoi reported to have been acted out by the dreamer.

For example, one Iroquoi brave dreamed that he had sex with another brave's wife. When he came out of the teepee, the other brave stabbed him in the chest with a knife, killing him (Ragueneau 1959). He went to the chief and told him his dream. The chief told him that he must act out his dream exactly like he dreamed it. He then went to the couple and told them his dream. The other brave waited outside the teepee while he had sex with the wife. When he came out of the teepee, the other brave stabbed him in the chest with a knife and killed him.

Another brave dreamed that he carried a little three-year-old girl, who he knew, into the woods and killed her. He went to the chief and told him his dream. The chief went and got the little girl and gave her to the brave. The chief told him that he must act out his dream exactly as he dreamed it. The brave then carried the little girl into the woods (Ragueneau 1959).

Although I believe much can be learned from acting out dreams, I consider these two examples to be a little extreme. However, there is no end to what religion can do.

Where did the Iroquoi come from? The Iroquoi believe that they have always been here, living around the Great Lakes and on both sides of the St. Lawrence River. However, genetic research shows that they are of Northern European ancestry (Sykes 2012). It is believed that their ancestors immigrated to America about 10,000 to 15,000 years ago from Northern Europe. They probably walked on a land and ice bridge. However, they may have immigrated by boat.

6
Temiar Senoi

The Temiar Senoi is a primitive tribe of approximately 12,000 people. They are one of three groups of aborigines living in the mountainous jungles on the peninsula of Malaysia. They live in extended family units in communal longhouses where each family has its own living compartment and cooks separately. The members of the longhouse interact like a village, using the central floor area as a street. They work a cleared area of jungle, which has rich soil for growing pumpkins, yams, bananas, rice, and tapioca. They stay as long as the land is fertile, then they move to a new area and clear the jungle off to create a new growing area with rich soil. It takes them one week to build a longhouse, which lasts six years, and another week to clear land for planting. Food cultivation and gathering require only a couple of hours each day. This allows them many leisure hours, which they devote to their dreams.

The Senoi are mostly vegetarians but also hunt animals with blowpipes. They also catch fish by using a fruit juice as a drug, causing the fish to float to the surface. They have only four numbers: one, two, three, and many.

They are reported to be individualistic, creative, and have extraordinary psychological adjustment. They show remarkable emotional maturity. They tolerate polygamy and polyandry in addition to the usual monogamy.

The Senoi believe that they possess several souls. The head-soul, which is the thinking soul, leaves the body on special errands or to gain experience. The liver-soul is primarily concerned with learning about the future. Other principal souls are the eye-soul, the breath-soul, and the heart-soul (Noone and Holman 1972; Benjamin 1969).

They are also animists and believe that the jungle is populated with spirits who haunt the rivers, streams, rock pools, rapids, river junctions, waterfalls, mountains, and other features. These spirits possess certain human attributes, but are more powerful and indestructible (Noone and Holman 1972).

During sleep, they believe their souls leave their body and interact with the spirits of the jungle. Their dreams are what they remember of these out-of-body experiences. They consider their dreams to be spiritual experiences as real and important as their waking life.

Every adult knows and practices dream interpretation, which is a daily feature of education and social intercourse. Breakfast is like a dream clinic with everyone telling, listening to, and analyzing dreams. Children listen to their parents' dreams from the night before and hear them criticized or congratulated for their actions during the dream. The children are then asked to report their dreams.

Children begin to report dreams as soon as they can talk.

Parents, grandparents, and older brothers and sisters all praise the child for remembering and reporting a dream. They ask about the child's behavior in the dream, point out wrong behavior, ask questions about past events relevant to the dream, suggest how to change behavior and attitude in future dreams, and finally recommend social actions based on the dream. These dream directions are closely linked with controlling the growth of the child's social consciousness. Living in a communal society, parents also teach children to be highly cooperative, saying "Cooperate with your fellows; if you must oppose their wishes, oppose them with goodwill" (Noone and Holman 1972).

The theme of dream advice is aggression, action, and to never be afraid. If the child advances boldly against dream monsters, dream animals, and dream ghosts and defeats them, with the help of relatives, dream friends, and friendly spirits, the monsters or ghosts become slaves. If the child runs away, these beings will plague the child until they are defeated. They believe violence in dreams to be very good in that only through violence can spirits be made to serve, and by killing them, their power to harm is destroyed. They also believe dream images can only be judged by their actions (Noone and Holman 1972).

The Senoi belief behind all this is that a person can only achieve power over the forces of evil if they have the courage to reach out boldly, and only then with the help of relatives, friends, and friendly spirits. An individual cannot do it alone, but is dependent on friends and relatives, as they are on him. If while awake, they help other people, they can ask for help from their souls while dreaming. Eventually a person should become the supreme ruler of his or her own dream or spiritual universe. In opposition to this, fear makes souls withdraw deep into the body, becoming repressed and paralyzed (Noone and Holman 1972).

Children are taught that adventure is very important in dreams. Whenever they dream of falling, flying, soaring, climbing, or traveling, they must let themselves go. These sensations are believed to be efforts of souls to get free of the body, and fear will only impede them (Noone and Holman 1972).

Children are encouraged by statements like: "That is a wonderful dream," "That is one of the best dreams a person can have," "Falling is the quickest way to gain power from the spirit world," and "The falling spirits love you and are attracting you to their land" (Tart 1972).

They are also asked questions like: "Where did you fall to?," "What did you discover?," and "What did you do?" In this way, over a period of time, dreams change from fear of falling into the joy of flying. This is what happens to every Senoi (Tart 1972).

After breakfast, most of the family members go to the village council where serious dream discussion continues with the larger group. Each person expresses his opinion of the meaning and significance of each image and situation. Those who agree on a meaning adopt it as a group project. Friendships are formed and activities organized to create costumes and paintings and do dances or sing songs from their dreams. Most of their daily activities are determined in this way. Dreams of the children are also discussed and considered to be as important as those of adults.

As Senoi children grow older, their dreams evolve. By adolescence, if they have the makings of a *halak* (a shamon or medicine man), they are dreaming of a recurring dream image, an attendant spirit called a *gunig*, which usually takes the shape of a tiger. The elders gauge the degree of their maturity as a *halak* by the actions and suggestions of their *gunig* (Noone & Holman 1972).

The *halak* is the link between the spirit world and his group. The principal function of his dance is religious in that through this, the *halak* and his *gunig* struggle together against the many evil spirits in nature.

At the end of the dance, the dancers suddenly collapse and lie on the floor in varying degrees of catatonia. When the trance subsides, the dancers wander about in a state of possession by the *gunig*. They blow and suck through clenched fists and utter spells in an unknown language and converse with spirits in the spirits own language. Occasionally an entranced dancer will act like a bird or animal because the forces of good and evil are struggling for possession (Noone and Holman 1972).

According to Kilton Stewart (1976,) Charles Tart (1972) and Patricia Garfield (1974,) the Senoi are a peaceful culture in which violence of any sort is extremely rare. They also contend that the Senoi maintain this peacefulness despite the warlike tribes nearby, which are fearful of what they regard as the magical power of the Senoi.

I don't believe the Senoi are all that peaceful and nonviolent. In Richard Noone's book *In Search of the Dream People* (Noone and Holman 1972) there are two reports of planned murder. There is also a picture of Senoi soldiers carrying rifles and fighting with communist forces against the Japanese during World War II.

I consider it very important to remember that the Senoi person is not entirely responsible for his crimes. If a Senoi commits a crime, all of his relatives are collectively accountable. This creates even more control, responsibility, guilt, shame, cover-up, and reluctance of admitting that there is ever any crime. If a Senoi mentions a crime, he is also responsible and accountable for it.

This was the reason Richard Noone had so much trouble finding out what had happened to his brother Pat. Hubert "Pat" Noone was the anthropologist who originally discovered and reported to the world about the Senoi and their dream methods in 1934. Pat married a Senoi and lived with them until his disappearance during World War II.

It took Richard Noone several years before a Senoi would tell him what had happened to Pat. A Senoi wanted Pat's wife and planned his murder. With a friend, he shot Pat with poison darts from a blowpipe, which paralyzed him. He then cut his throat with a machete. The killer later married Pat's wife. All of the Senoi felt responsible, guilty, and ashamed. Therefore, they would not even mention Pat's name and tried to forget about him. It is kind of ironic that the man who discovered and reported these "peaceful" Senoi to the world was killed by a Senoi for his wife.

I consider the Senoi and their approach to dreams to be very important in that:

1. They demonstrate that dreaming is a creative process with choice.
2. People do dream according to their belief system.

3. Dreaming can be educational.
4. Dreaming can improve communication and relations with others.
5. Using dreams, children are taught never to be afraid or to avoid. They are also taught to move toward aggression and action.

The following are a few objections I have to the Senoi approach:
1. Their approach is connected with their religion. They are animists and believe that they have several souls including a group soul that protects them from evil spirits.
2. The basis of their approach is their belief in the out-of-body experience. They believe that their souls leave their bodies during sleep and interact with each other and with the souls of rocks, streams, animals, etc. In this way, they believe their dreams to be actual experiences of their souls.
3. Dream directions are closely linked with the growth of social consciousness.
4. Their approach is extremely controlling as opposed to the Iroquois approach, which I consider to be extremely freeing.

Passivity has become a disease in our culture. I believe people would be less passive if they had been taught never to avoid and always to move toward aggression and action while dreaming.

David Wallin (1977) successfully improved five out of

eight subjects' dreaming by teaching them a three-point distillation of Senoi: confront danger, approach pleasure, and achieve positive outcomes in dreams.

I consider this to be outstanding in that he has demonstrated that persons in our society can be taught how to improve their dreaming. I also believe that any changes in dreaming may carry over into the dreamer's waking life.

7
Sigmund Freud
1856-1939

In the late 1800s there were three main views on dreams: the external forces view, that dreams were both from God and the devil; the physiological view, that dreams were caused by physical sensations of the body during sleep, such as temperature, indigestion, etc.; and the third view, that dreams were meaningless.

Freud kept an extensive dream journal, which he destroyed along with his diaries in April 1885 when he was twenty-eight (Diamond 1963). My fantasy is that he did not want them read by others. His stated reason was that, "The stuff simply enveloped me as the sand does the Sphinx." If this were true, he could have just stopped recording his dreams without destroying his journal. Freud had his own views on dreams and wrote *The Interpretation of Dreams* (1965) first published November 1899 (dated 1900) for which he received a total of $250. This book remained his favorite throughout his life and he wrote that it contained "the most valuable of all discoveries it has been my good fortune to make. Insight such as this falls to one's lot but once in a lifetime" (Faraday 1973).

Freud's book was so radical that it was treated with contempt and dismissed as a mixture of obscenity and obscurity. For this reason it sold only 600 copies the first eight years. It eventually became popular and emphasis in thought on the dream shifted from the physiological and external to the psychological experience.

Freud's dream approach is based on the same principle as his whole psychological theory. That concept is that we all have strivings, unwanted ideas, feelings, and wishes that are unknown to us, yet motivate our actions. He called this unknown the "unconscious," a phrase used in intellectual circles in Germany as early as the late eighteenth century (Regush and Regush 1977). The only difference is that up until Freud, "unconscious" was only used as an adjective and Freud used it as a noun.

According to Freud, a powerful "censor" protects us from knowing what is in our "unconscious," impulses whose existence we do not want nor dare not recognize when we are awake (Fromm 1951). Freud believed that the dream came from the "unconscious," which is beyond our reach when awake.

I reject this whole idea that we are protected from knowing what is in our own minds by a powerful "censor," from impulses whose existence we do not want nor dare recognize. Just what could possibly be so devastating that we must be protected from it? The "unconscious" is only a word used to disown responsibility or to explain anything unknown. The biggest problem is that its definition and content have varied so much from one author to another (De Becker 1968). I believe that it is best to abandon such a vague and varied label.

A second assumption Freud makes about dreams is that they come from what he called "the prehistoric period," the ages one to three. During "the prehistoric period" we behaved principally on the basis of what felt good to us without social constraints (Cartwright 1977).

He believed that what was seen during ages one to three "gives rise to" dreams. What was heard during ages one to three "gives rise to" fantasies and what was sexually experienced during ages one to three "gives rise to" psychoneurosis (Cartwright 1977; Diamond 1963).

Freud discounted everything other than what was seen during ages one to three. He believed that every dream could be traced back to what was seen in ages one to three.

I reject this completely. There is no reason to trace dreams back to any time. This suggests that we have no choice or control over what we dream. I would guess from this that if a person could be totally isolated or kept unconscious and alive until age four, they would never dream. Freud was also unaware that every person dreams most, if not all, of the time they are asleep; far more time is spent dreaming than the entire time awake during the ages of one to three. If a person lived to age seventy and dreamed only seven hours a night, minus ages one to three, that person would dream 365 days multiplied by seven hours of sleep a day multiplied by sixty-seven years equals 171,185 hours of dreaming. Three years multiplied by seventeen hours awake equals 18,615 hours awake during ages one to three. If you divide 171,185 by 18,615, it equals 9.8, or in other words, everything seen during ages one to three could be dreamed at least 9.8 times.

As far as the "seen" is concerned, this suggests that persons who were blind during ages one to three do not dream because they did not see anything. Of course, this is not true—blind people do dream. However, some of them dream without visual imagery (Dement and Kleitman 1957).

Freud believed that dreams have two purposes. The first is to allow repressed wishes from ages one to three, mostly of a sexual nature, to obtain fulfillment and satisfaction in the form of a dream. These unacceptable desires run counter to the dreamer's internalized value system and must be disguised to prevent disturbing the dreamer and waking him up. We imagine our infantile desires have been fulfilled and feel satisfied rather than a disturbing frustration. Therefore, Freud's second purpose of dreams is to preserve or guard sleep (Freud 1962, 1965).

I consider the wish-fulfillment theory too narrow a construct for understanding the function of the dream. I agree with Fritz Perls that all dreams can be divided into two groups, those that are wish-fulfillments and those that are not wish-fulfillments. Of course, dreams can be divided this way for any theory, those dreams that fit the theory and those that do not fit the theory. Along this line, Freud himself later divided dreams into two groups, wish-fulfillment dreams and counter-wish dreams. He described counter-wish dreams as coming from two sources: "mental masochists" and the wish that he (Freud) may be wrong (Freud 1962, 1965).

Freud's suggestion that the second purpose of dreams is to preserve or guard sleep seems to be a paradox, because some people are often awakened by their dreams. Freud was aware of this and eventually revised his theory to say that the dream was an "attempted wish-fulfillment."

Also, Freud was unaware that dreaming takes place during most, if not all, of sleep. It seems more reasonable to believe that sleep preserves dreaming.

Freud assumed that the dream is always "stimulated" by a present event, usually on the day or evening before sleep. The dream is only "provoked" by such events that are related to the "infantile" wish. The energy for the dream stems from the intensity of the "infantile" experience.

Freud assumed that, while wishes from ages one to three are activated by events of the day, they are prevented from entering consciousness during waking life by what he called the "repression barrier." During sleep, this barrier is weaker, allowing wishes to enter consciousness in the form of a disguised dream.

Since Freud considered that repressed "infantile" wishes in the "unconscious" found substitute gratification during waking life in the form of symptoms and during sleep in the form of dreams, he therefore considered the dream to be a neurotic symptom (Faraday 1973).

I disagree that all dreams are neurotic symptoms. In my opinion, some are, but most dreams are expressive of health. I see dreams as being expressive of the dreamer. To say that dreams are neurotic symptoms would be to say that dreamers are neurotic. Since every person dreams, this would indicate that every person is neurotic. I contend that most persons are healthy and therefore most dreams are expressive of health.

He was not aware of how much dreaming every person

does every night, nor did he see dreams used for anything other than psychoanalysis.

Freud made more use of accidental symbols than universal symbols and held that in order to interpret a dream we have to:
1. Cut the dream up into pieces and do away with its sequence.
2. Associate to each element and substitute the thoughts that come to mind.
3. Put together all these thoughts that come to mind and arrive at a new text, which has consistency, logic, and divulges the true meaning (Fromm 1951).

In doing this, Freud was only applying to dreams the methods he used in the treatment of phobias, obsessions, and other symptoms (De Becker 1968). According to Jung, Freud used the dream only as a beginning point from which the dreamer eventually unraveled his own neurosis through free association. Jung suggested that almost any statement or idea could serve as a starting point for free association (O'Nell 1976).

This new text, which divulges the true meaning or repressed wish from ages one to three, Freud called "latent dream." The dream, as it was originally remembered by the dreamer, he called the "manifest dream." The process of disguising the "latent dream" into the "manifest dream" he called the "dream-work." The main mechanisms of "dream-work" are:
1. "Condensation," which is the mechanism by which several "latent dream" ideas are condensed into a single image in the "manifest dream." These ideas do not need to be related.

2. "Dramatization," which is the mechanism by which one "latent dream" idea is dramatized into several images and/or situations in the "manifest dream."
3. "Displacement," which is the mechanism that attaches the emotion really connected with one situation to a very different one in order to distract attention from the actual object of the feelings. Also, when a "latent dream" idea, often a very important one, is expressed by a remote element in the "manifest dream," it is usually one that appears unimportant.
4. "Symbolization," which is the mechanism by which "latent dream" ideas are represented by a substitute object, idea, or symbol in the "manifest dream."
5. "Secondary elaboration," which is the mechanism that completes the process of disguise. Gaps are filled in and inconsistencies are repaired with the result of forming a logical consistent story as a disguise.
6. "Secondary revision," which is the natural tendency to make sense of the dream while remembering it on waking.

Freud believed that the symbolic language of a dream cannot express any kind of feeling or thought, but can only disguise an "infantile" wish. For this reason, he has been greatly criticized for giving too little credence to the importance of the "manifest dream" (Faraday 1973).

In considering the dream as remembered only to be a disguise, Freud refused to see the dream as a creative expression. I agree with both Jung and Perls that if we look at a dream very closely, everything is there. A dream is a creative expression of the dreamer about himself. There is no reason to disguise anything. Freud, in believing the dream to be a disguise, was only projecting his lack of understanding. Dreams are like paintings. A painting is not a disguise, but is creative and revealing. If I do not see what the artist is trying to reveal, that does not mean the painting is a disguise.

Although Freud stated that some dreams satisfy needs other than sexual, he saw most symbols to be of a sexual nature. To Freud, the male genital is symbolized by objects, which can represent it either by their shape or by their function. Examples are sticks, trees, umbrellas, knives, pencils, hammers, airplanes, snakes, keys, spires, and bananas. The female genital is represented in the same manner. Examples are caves, bottles, boxes, doors, ovens, jewel cases, gardens, flowers, locks, pockets, holes, gates, ships, and all kinds of vessels. Sexual pleasure is represented by activities like dancing, flying, climbing, and riding. Falling is anxiety about giving into eroticism. Castration fears and the inevitable punishment for having masturbated are represented by the falling out of hair or teeth.

To Freud, symbols are also disguises for fundamental experiences of the little child. Father and mother are symbolized as king and queen or emperor and empress, children as little animals, and death as a journey (Calogeras 1977).

I also believe that Freud's male supremacy attitude carried over into his dream theory. In *The Interpretation of Dreams* he referred to women as the passive sex, suckler of babies, and physically clumsy (Calogeras 1977).

Freud himself was not an orthodox Freudian. Accounts he gave of his own and his patients' dreams rarely go back to sexual experiences during ages one to three. He rationalized the fact that many of his accounts stop short at an unconscious wish from adult experience by saying that interpretation could be possible at several levels. However, his overall approach seems to indicate that "unknown" wishes from ages one to three are unpleasant, anxiety-producing, and have sexual overtones (Faraday 1973; Regush and Regush 1977).

David Foulkes (1962, 1964) and Gerald Vogel (1960) have done extensive research on sleep and dreams in laboratories. Their laboratory findings, and those of others, disagree with Freud's concept of the role of preconscious factors in dreaming. They have called for a revision of Freud's theory and other theories based on this premise. Raymond Fancher and Robert Strahan (1971) have also partially disproved Freud's dream theory.

Although Freud's approach to dreams seems of little value, he did make two great contributions. The first was that of attracting interest away from the external and physiological approaches to the psychological approach to dreams. The other was that the Freudian approach to dreams served as an evolutionary link to modern dream approaches.

Jung and Perls both practiced the Freudian approach to dreams before evolving their own approaches. Both hung on to "free association," "identification," "transference," and "projection." They improved on these constructs and evolved them into their own styles.

The main reason I included the Freudian approach to dreams is that it is the one most believed by the average person. Although the average person believes the Freudian approach to dreams, most are misinformed as to what it is.

I believe that informing people as to what the Freudian approach to dreams is will be enough to change their opinion.

Most people seem to forget that the Freudian approach is 1900 Vienna. Both people and society are different now. Psychology and approaches to dreams have evolved a great deal since 1900.

In a way, I feel very close to Freud. He exaggerated his approach as a reaction against the anti-sexual Victorian Vienna of 1900. I am exaggerating my approach as a reaction against the Freudian anti-choice, anti-responsibility, and anti-creativity of our sick Victorian society of today.

8
Carl Jung
1875 - 1961

Jung (1974) de-emphasized the significance of sex and denied wish-fulfillment, censorship, and the dream as guardian of sleep.

I agree with his view of dreams as normal, natural events, which can be creative and expressive of health as well as pathology. Jung (1933) believed, as do I, that the human body has an inbuilt tendency toward psychological health and dreams are a part of that system. To him, the dream is a perfect expression and we should learn to listen to our dreams. He considered the dream to be an expression of the wisdom of the unconscious, a concept that I personally do not use.

Jung (1938, 1974) considered the unconscious to be capable of assuming an intelligence and purpose superior to actual conscious insight. He believed this to be a "basic religious phenomenon" from a source transcending us.

Like the unresolved sexual problem in the background of Freud's theories, there is an unresolved religious problem in the background of Jung's theories. Jung's education and his own thinking about religion allowed him to reject the dogma of his father's Christianity, yet the effect of his childhood Christian training hung on, and he kept his Christian belief by seeing it "in a new light" and changed it to fit his belief system. He felt extremely misunderstood by the religious thinkers of his time, who interpreted his writings to be anti-Christian, when in his opinion they were a contribution to Christianity.

I believe Jung had an unresolved religious problem as evidenced by his failure to keep his religion out of his approach to dreams. I look upon his use of religious assumptions as imposing his own faith on his patients (Jung 1965).

Jung did not give a precise definition for "archetypal images," which has resulted in many people misunderstanding what he meant. This has left "archetypal images" as an ambiguous concept. Some people have interpreted archetypes to be images acquired during evolution and transmitted through the genes of our species. I believe Jung did not mean that images are inherited, but the potential for forming such images may result from a common inheritance (O'Nell 1976). When the dreamer is unable to find personal associations, Jung suggests that interpretation might be found in terms of the archetypes.

Jung (1974) believed that dreams restore psychological balance to the dreamer by presenting the other side or opposite of one's personality or life situation. In sort, dreams compensate for deficiencies in the life situation and warn about the danger of imbalance.

There is an excellent outline of the Jungian approach to dream interpretation in Mary Ann Mattoon's book *Applied*

Dream Analysis: A Jungian Approach. If you are interested in the Jungian approach, I suggest you look at that outline on pages forty-eight and forty-nine (Mattoon 1978).

Recent experimental studies have failed to find any compensatory aspects of dreams or fantasies. The findings reflect a commonality of themes in both the dream reports and the dreamer's personality. The results clearly indicate that, according to Domino: "What occurs in dreams is not substantially different from what occurs in conscious thought" (Domino 1976; Palmiere 1972).

9
B. F. Skinner
1904 - 1990

Skinner has not applied his approach to dreams in any detail. He has explicitly stated that he agrees with the basic features of Freud's approach to dreams (Chandra 1976; Skinner 1953; Skinner 1974; Boring 1950). This fits in very well with his statement: "In some sense we are all Freudians" (Chandra 1976; Skinner, 1972).

This seems surprising, yet Skinner and Freud are in agreement on many issues. Both are strict determinists. Both belong to what is called the "functional" tradition in psychology (Boring 1950). Both constructed their systems without resorting to physiological variables. They agree on the priority of environmental over hereditary explanation for any given feature of behavior (Chandra 1976; Freud 1962; Freud 1963; Skinner 1969).

For Skinner, as for Freud, behavior is fundamentally unconscious and "the only problem is consciousness." They see "consciousness" as the exception rather than the rule, which arises only as a result of social experience (Brenner 1974; Chandra 1976; Skinner 1969).

Of course, alongside all these similarities, some differences do exist. However, considerable regard for the contributions of Freud, particularly his understanding of human behavior, is scattered throughout Skinner's work (Chandra 1976; Evans and Skinner 1968; Singer and Antrobus 1963; Skinner 1972; Skinner 1974).

The few instances in which Skinner mentions dreams, he simply replaces some of the Freudian labels with his own labels; for example, "condensation" becomes "minimal repertoire" and "meaning" becomes "controlling relation." He also refers to Freud's approach using terms such as: primary reinforces, conditioned responses, controlling variables, discriminative stimuli, abstraction, autoclitic behavior, and atomic operants (Chandra 1976; Skinner 1953; Skinner 1957; Skinner 1974).

I disagree with Skinner's approach (and Freud's) in many ways. I do not see human behavior as determined by the environment. I do not see human behavior as determined by the "unconscious" resulting from ages one to three. I see behavior as both genetic and as a "conscious" choice; I choose my environment.

10
Transactional Analysis

Arthur Samuels (1974), who takes a TA approach, defines a dream as "a dynamic symbolic representation of a person's existential position within a life script."

First, he says, the dreamer re-experiences the dream by relating it in the present tense. Second, the dreamer identifies with each part of the dream and assigns it an ego state role (parent, adult, or child). Third, the dreamer role-plays the parts of the dream. An alternative approach is for the group members to play the parts.

Shepard Gellert (1975) uses dreams to gain understanding of script protocol and early script scenes. After making a contract, the "patient is asked to be a part of the dream (to establish an age or feeling) and to go with the feeling or action of the dream (as a "rubber band") to an early scene and decision."

The TA approach to dreams seems similar to the Gestalt approach. For this reason, I prefer the TA approach over those discussed so far. However, the TA approach seems very past-oriented, as though dreams arrive from unfinished past experiences. This is not surprising, considering that TA is another form of analysis that evolved from the Freudian approach.

# 11
Carl Rogers
1902-1987

Carl Rogers believed that every organism is born with a genetic blueprint. He believed that the goal of life is to fulfill that genetic blueprint, which he called the "actualizing tendency." Humans also developed images of themselves that closely match their genetic blueprint. Striving to fulfill our self-image of ourselves, he called the "self-actualizing tendency." When our self-image of ourselves closely matches our genetic blueprint we become a "fully functioning person." According to Rogers (1961), people become more fully functioning when they are raised by parents that give them "unconditional positive regard." However, most parents do not accept their children the way they are and try to change their children to be the way they want them. Teachers, friends, relatives, and religion also try to change the person to become and behave the way they want. Rogers referred to this as "conditional positive regard." This is the tendency of parents to give their children love and affection only as long as the child's behavior is approved by the parent. Some parents even believe that it is their duty to "raise" a child to be the way they want that child to become. In the process, the gap between the child's self-concept and the child's genetic blueprint widens and the child becomes less and less like their genetic blueprint (Rogers 1961, 1980, 2003).

When people lose sight of their genetic blueprint they feel frustrated because they have become what other people wanted them to become instead of becoming the way they wanted to come. Eventually, they will realize they don't know who they are (Morris and Maisto 2010). I consider psychotherapy to be the act of letting go of all those things that separate us from our genetic blueprint.

Rogers called his therapy "client-centered" because he placed the responsibility for change on the client. Rogers was non-directive and tried to understand things from the viewpoint of the client. Rogers was big on reflection because many people do not hear what they are saying; they just talk. Saying back to the person what they just said is a way for them to hear what they are saying.

Carl Rogers has made a far greater contribution to psychotherapy than most people realize. I appreciate him more and more every day.

12
Fritz Perls
1893 - 1970

Fritz Perls, the founder of Gestalt Therapy, rejected the theory of "the unconscious." He thought of the personality as a ball floating and turning in water, with only one portion visible at a time and all portions visible at different times. He worked with that portion which is visible and focused his attention on the actual behavior of the person. He did this in order to discover the "holes" in the personality caused by the rejection of certain parts in order to avoid pain. He watched how the person avoided the present and guided him or her to act out painful situations to reintegrate the disowned parts of his or her personality. He preferred working with dreams and called the dream "the royal road to integration." In other words, he believed that a dream is a "clear existential message" of what the dreamer is avoiding.

Perls regarded every part of the dream, including the environment, as a disowned part of the dreamer, which has been projected onto that image. He rejected the whole idea of repression and considered it to be total nonsense. He did that because, if we look, especially in dreams, everything is there, projected all over the place. Because of our avoidance of awareness and pain, we disown many parts of ourselves. In this way, most of our potential is unavailable to us. Perls believed that we attempt to make this disowned potential available to us by using projection.

Dreams are very handy to work with the projected parts of our selves. By working with every item in a dream as a projected disowned part of the dreamer, the dreamer can re-own that part and gain more of his or her potential.

In order to do this, Perls first has the dreamer tell the dream as though he or she is experiencing it now, first person, present tense. In this way the dreamer re-lives the dream more fully. He next has the dreamer "set the stage," showing where each part is, as though he or she is experiencing it here and now. He then has the dreamer become each part, experiencing that part of himself more fully by acting out its role in the dream. The dreamer also talks about him or herself as each part. He then has the dreamer create a dialogue or encounter between all the parts.

Perls considered it unnecessary to work with every part of the dream, as long as the dreamer was able to find at least one existential message from the dream. The aim is to re-own and bring the fragmented parts of the personality into harmony with each other to facilitate growth.

I disagree with Perls that all the parts of the dream are unacceptable (disowned) parts of the dreamer. My dreams contain both acceptable (owned) parts as well as unacceptable (disowned) parts. I believe Perls held to unacceptable (disowned) parts for four reasons: first, so that working with dreams fit in with his entire approach to therapy—and more specifically, fit in with reintegration of disowned parts of the personality. Second, Perls seemed unaware that dreamers "consciously" create and manipulate dreams. Third, he tried to fit dreams into a simple theory similar to Freud's wish fulfillment theory. Fourth, projection of unacceptable (disowned) parts attempts to explain the function of dreaming.

When working with dreams for therapy in a private session, one client and one therapist, I consider Fritz Perls's method to be the best. However, Perls preferred working with one person at a time in a group setting, one person acting out his or her dream with several persons watching. I agree that this method is very therapeutic for the dreamer, but what about the other group participants? Therapeutic or not, as a participant, I soon get very bored watching one person working alone on a dream.

13
My View of Gestalt Therapy

Gestalt Therapy has very little to do with Gestalt psychology, which is concerned with perception (Shepard 1975). Gestalt Therapy does focus on how people perceive themselves and their environment.

Perls chose the term "Gestalt" over "Existential" Therapy and "Concentration" Therapy, which he preferred. He did this for the following reasons:

1. Gestalt psychology had a good growing reputation and people might have connected the two, which would have helped it become more popular.
2. Perls's wife, Laura, was traditionally trained as a Gestalt psychologist and he could use this as a reason.
3. He wanted a title that would sell and be remembered.
4. Perhaps because of his German background he chose a German word.

My personal preference would have been to label it

Existential Therapy and let the therapy do the selling rather than the label.

The first basic premise of Gestalt is homeostasis or organismic self-regulation. The homeostatic process is the process by which the organism interacts with its environment and satisfies its needs. Since there are many needs and each upsets the equilibrium, homeostasis is a continual process. Life is characterized by this continuing balance and imbalance. Every person has thousands of psychological needs in addition to thousands of physiological needs.

I like thinking of each need as a rubber band attached to a centering point; right of this is minus and left of this point is a plus. An example of a physiological need could be water. As I become thirsty, I move to the right of center, slightly off balance. The longer I stop myself from drinking water, the more off balance or right of center I become. Due to my excessive thirst, I drink a little too much and move left of center, slightly off balance on the plus side, until I have gone without water long enough to become centered and balanced as far as my need for water is concerned.

Psychological needs can also be seen graphically in a similar way. For example, if my need for touch was off center on the minus side, I might choose to attend a weekend massage workshop. At first I would feel great touching and being touched by others. I can imagine possibly becoming balanced by the end of the first day. On the second day I could possibly move to the left of center and far enough unbalanced that I wouldn't want to be touched for a while until I became more centered.

All of this is a good way to explain needs, which are a

reality. However, I consider it better to just forget about all these needs. I prefer to say that all needs are self-regulating, therefore I can forget about them; they take care of themselves. When I'm thirsty, I drink. When I'm hungry, I eat. When I need a relationship, I find a relationship. The only problem arises when I stop myself.

Therefore, most Gestalt Therapy is focused on "How I am stopping myself," and learning ways to not stop myself—to simply allow myself to live. I am free to do anything I want to. Therefore, I can find out what I want by watching what I do. Most people seem to first decide what they want to do and then try to achieve that. This is the reason most people are future oriented. Watching what I am doing is a now experience.

During the first eighteen years or so of life, a person is forced to swallow whole the ideas, beliefs, and "should" of parents, teachers, and our sick society. Perls described the process of maturation as regurgitating all these ideas, beliefs, and "shoulds," chewing them up, spitting out what we don't want, and swallowing only what is wanted. This becomes another focus of Gestalt Therapy. These unwanted ideas, beliefs, and "shoulds," are the main cause of my stopping myself, which in turn causes me to become unbalanced.

Another approach is to change language. The idea is that by changing the way I talk, I will also change the way I think and the way I perceive myself and my environment. This is done by changing:

- It" to "I"
- You" to "I"
- We" to "I"
- Can't" to "Won't"

- Need" to "Want"
- Have to" to "Choose to"
- Know" to "Imagine"
- But" to "And"
- Questions to Statements
- Passive voice to Active voice

Although I understand that this can be very useful, I am moving away from changing language. I believe this contributes to "psychobabble" and creates friction and lack of communication with those who "normal speak."

The following are some of the assumptions Gestalt Therapy makes:

1. Man is neither good nor bad.
2. Change takes place through frustration.
3. Awareness by and of itself can be curative (Perls 1969).
4. I do what I want to.
5. I can find out what I want by watching what I do.

Gestalt Therapy focuses on:

1. Awareness of here and now.
2. Exaggeration.
3. Fantasy.
4. Letting go of goals.
5. Letting go of the future and past.
6. Choice.
7. Responsibility.
8. Nonverbal behavior.
9. Body language.
10. Projection.
11. Presenting the past and future.

12. Feelings.
13. Avoidance.
14. Acceptance.

The interested reader will find further information about this list in each of Perls last three books (Perls 1969a; Perls 1969b; Perls 1973) and many other Gestalt-oriented books (Downing 1973; Fagan and Shepherd 1970; Fagan and Shephard 1971; Kroon 1972; Latner 1974; Passons 1975; Polster and Polster 1973; Rosenblatt 1975; Simkin 1976; Smith 1977; Stevens 1977; Zinker 1978). There are many Gestalt Therapy techniques. The most well-known is that of offering the client the opportunity to have a dialogue between two parts of the client by talking to an empty chair or pillows. In this way the client more fully experiences feelings and increases awareness. I usually include a third part, which is the part of the client that knows all the alternatives.

I often use several pillows to represent several different parts of the client or the client's significant others, such as mother, father, brothers, sisters, lovers, grandparents, boss, coworkers, children, friends, etc. I have the client play the part of each, having a dialogue and changing from pillow to pillow. I stay out of the dialogue, observing and guiding only when the client is stuck or getting off track. This technique also relies heavily on the client's own projections. I believe this to be superior to Psychodrama, which is contaminated by the feelings, perceptions, projections, etc. of other participants.

I have experienced many different therapies and found Gestalt Therapy to be the best for my own growth. I believe Psychoanalysis would take years to achieve the growth results of only a few months of Gestalt Therapy. I have attended several Bioenergetics groups and the only thing I was aware of was being sweaty. If a body therapy is preferred, Neo-Reichian Therapy can be combined with Gestalt Therapy. Eric Marcus, MD, does an excellent job of combining Neo-Reichian Therapy with Gestalt Therapy and I am sure many others do also.

I once asked Eric Marcus, MD, what the difference is between Reichian Therapy and Neo-Reichian Therapy. He said, "Neo-Reichians let you keep your underpants on." Of course this was a joke that I thought was very funny.

14
My Approach to Therapy

I was in the Freeman Institute Facilitators Training Program for about six years. The program was directed by Albert V. Freeman, PhD, and Evelyn L. Freeman, PhD, MFCC. The training consisted of every style and modality the leaders were trained in, plus many guest therapists demonstrating their approaches. Therefore, I considered the training to be eclectic and very unique.

My own style of therapy is eclectic and similar to that of the two leaders, yet different. If I had to choose only one therapy, I would choose Gestalt Therapy. I do not have to make that choice, and therefore consider Gestalt to be only one of many therapies I use. I believe Gestalt is important to know, yet when it comes time to do therapy, I consider it better to keep it "in the back of my mind."

I have been trained to "stay with" and "follow" the client. I work with what the client says and does. I do not mention dreams unless the client mentions a dream. I listen "creatively" and watch for "key words" and physical

movements. I share my feelings and I make the following assumptions:
1. The client is already the way he or she wants to be.
2. The client is already doing what he or she wants to do.
3. The client already knows all the answers and all the alternatives.
4. All feelings are positive. A feeling usually considered "unwanted," such as feeling depressed, is positive, in that it gets me to do something different.
5. Feelings are chosen, usually by creating a statement and sometimes followed by a prediction. I can change that feeling by changing the statement.
6. In this way, the client is choosing to feel the way he or she wants to feel.
7. I "go with" the client's fantasy rather than showing the client reality as I see it.
8. Whatever the client is doing, it's a positive thing in that people only do things for positive reasons, usually to get something they want or to protect themselves.

In this way, I facilitate clients in discovering their responsibility in creating their lives. By taking responsibility for creating their lives, they become aware that they are in complete control of their lives and life situations. This, in turn, allows them to see alternatives and become more creative.

15
My Approach to Dreams

As I have shown in the first chapter, people in all stages of sleep are capable of dreaming. Also, dreams do not arise as isolated mental productions. Instead, there seems to be a continuation of dream theme content throughout sleep. Each stage of sleep continues the dream theme of the preceding stage. There is also continuity in waking and dream experience with some direct and indirect incorporation of daily interactions (Goodenough 1975; Kroon 1972).

My personal observation is that what I am thinking from the time I go to bed until the time I fall asleep is carried over into my dreaming. This is of particular interest to those who report having unpleasant dreams. I believe a person who reports having unpleasant dreams can change the content or quality of dreaming by using visual imagery just prior to sleep, which carries over into dreaming. By using visual imagery prior to sleep, or at any time during the day, a person may learn actively to create imagery the way he or she prefers it, rather than passively observing dreams.

I agree with Jung that dreams are creative and expressive and that the human body has an inbuilt tendency toward psychological health, and dreaming is a part of that system.

Belief greatly influences what and how a person dreams in the same way that it does in waking life. If a person believes a certain religion, they will live their lives and dream accordingly. In the same way, I believe that when people take responsibility for their lives and choose to live their lives exactly the way they want to, they also dream accordingly.

I consider it most important for the dreamer to take responsibility for his or her dreams. Most approaches to dreams disown or discount the dreamer's responsibility. A major example is the Freudian approach, in which events of the day stimulate wish-fulfillments from ages one to three which are "unconscious" and unknown to the dreamer. I see this as a way of avoiding responsibility.

I totally reject the whole idea of the "unconscious." The "unconscious" is only a theory. No one has ever proven that there is an "unconscious," or even where in the brain it is located. I don't know of any studies that have shown that when a certain portion of the brain is destroyed the person no longer has an "unconscious." I basically see the word "unconscious" as used to explain anything unknown. That's the reason I prefer to replace the word "unconscious" with the word "unknown."

I consider many therapists guilty of using the word "unconscious" to convince their clients that they, the therapists, know more about the clients than the clients know about themselves, because they, the clients, are controlled by "the unconscious." Then they confuse clients even further, by telling them there is supposed to be, according to Jung, "a collective unconscious."

Of course, all this plays right into the hands of the clients who want to disown their responsibility. Most people go into therapy wanting to believe that they are not responsible for their lives. They are eager to believe that they have no control, or have little control over significant behavior. Since their unconscious was formed during ages one to three, their parents are responsible for their lives being the way they are.

I consider it far more therapeutic to believe that I am responsible for my life and my dreams. Rather than looking for causes of my dreams, I take responsibility for creating my dreams. I am responsible for creating my dreams. And, since I am the one responsible, I can create them anyway I choose. Therefore, I create all of my dreams exactly the way I want them. I generalize this by saying that every person creates all of their dreams exactly the way they want them. Although I believe all dreams are created exactly the way the dreamer wants them, many people are unaware that they are doing this. It is important for every dreamer, at least once, to achieve an awareness of dreaming while dreaming, and manipulate the dream however they choose. This is done in order to take control and experience manipulating the dream while dreaming, and to realize that you not only can do this anytime you want, but that you have been doing this all along. I have found in my own personal experience that the easiest way to do this is to stay awake as long as possible, thirty-six to forty-eight hours or more, and then sleep as long as possible, sixteen hours or more. I have not found any evidence in the research literature that this could be harmful in any way.

It has been my impression that people vary a great deal in their use of imagery. Those who use, and are more creative using, imagery while awake are more creative during dreaming. The less creative they are using imagery while awake, the less imagery will appear in their dreams.

The uses of dreams I have become aware of include: learning, writing, communicating, therapy, self-awareness, entertainment, enjoyment, a way of sharing myself with someone, a way to get acquainted, an excuse or reason to bring a group of people together, a way to create a closer family, and possibly others.

16
How to Use Dreams in Therapy

I like comparing a dream with a painting. An artist paints a painting as a creative, expressive, and enjoyable experience. He chooses what to paint, what colors he is using, and where each color goes. The artist does not typically ask himself, "What is the meaning of this?" or "Why am I doing this?" The artist simply paints.

Similarly, dreaming is a creative, expressive, and enjoyable experience. The dreamer consciously chooses what to dream, what colors to use, and where everything goes in the dream. Dreaming is a now experience with choices being made every second.

If an artist decides he needs therapy, he might choose to carry his painting to a Gestalt art therapist. In the therapy sessions, the therapist will probably use projection techniques such as:

    1. Asking the artist to become the painting and talk about himself as that painting.

2. Asking the artist to become each object in the painting and talk about himself as that object.
3. Asking the artist to become each color and say how he feels as that color.

Each of these techniques relies on the artist to project his thoughts and feelings onto the painting. His becoming the painting or object facilitates his experience. This is all done in order to increase the artist's awareness of how he is feeling, thinking, avoiding, stopping himself, etc.

If a person decides she needs therapy and goes to a therapist, the therapist will ask about a dream. A Gestalt Therapist will probably use projection techniques such as:

1. Asking her to become the environment in which the dream action takes place and talk about herself as the environment.
2. Asking her to become an image in the dream and talk about herself as that image.
3. Asking her to become each color and say how she feels as the color.
4. Continuing to focus in this way on every aspect of the dream.

These techniques, like those of the art therapist, facilitate her experience and increase her awareness of how she is feeling, thinking, avoiding, stopping herself, etc.

I am making this comparison to show that the purpose of dreaming is not therapy. Dreams are just very useful to use for projection as a therapy. Also, a study by Michael Davies indicated that the initial dream is both diagnostic and prognostic (Passons 1975).

When working with one person in a private session, my approach is very similar to, and different from, that of Perls:

1. First, the dreamer tells the dream in first person, present tense. This is done to re-experience the dream in the "here and now."
2. The second step is what Perls refers to as "setting the stage." I have the dreamer arrange pillows around the room, placing them where that part or image in the dream was, using the room to represent the environment of the dream.
3. The dreamer and I discuss which parts seem to be best to work with. I prefer three parts; two is good. If the client has a multiple personality, such as believing he or she is two persons, I include those personalities as well as the two or three dream parts. If the dreamer is having trouble with a relationship, I sometimes include the other person also. Of course, it is better to use every part of the dream, but that is very time consuming.
4. The dreamer then becomes each of these dream parts and talks about himself as that part while acting like that part. I make sure that the dreamer states at least one feeling for each part. If the dreamer finishes with a part without a feeling, I point this out by saying, "I didn't hear you say how you are feeling as that part."
5. The dreamer is then instructed to have an encounter between all these parts, staying in role as each part of the dream, interacting with all the other selected parts. I prefer that the dreamer physically move from

pillow to pillow while talking as each part that the pillows represent.
6. I then have the dreamer act out the dream and ask how he or she is feeling.
7. Next, I ask the dreamer, "What was the purpose of your choosing to create this dream?"
8. I next ask the dreamer to change the dream to exactly the way he or she wants to dream it next time. Although this is most useful for recurring dreams, it also reinforces changing and creating dreams. It is my impression that about half refuse to change the dream, saying that it is already exactly the way they want it. This shows them that they are already creating their dreams exactly the way they want them.

I am often amused when a person starts out with what they call a "nightmare" and then at this point refuses to change it because they like it this way.

9. If time permits, have the dreamer rewrites the dream the way he or she wants to dream it next time and we can go back through steps 1 to 7 again. The dreamer tells the new dream, first person, present tense, etc.

When using a dream for therapy, I consider, as Fritz Perls did, every part of the dream to be a part of the dreamer, including objects, people, environment, feelings, sounds, time, speed, color, etc. It seems very easy to forget, yet very important to remember, that every part of the dream is a part of the dreamer.

I remember once participating in a group in which a woman, about eighteen years of age, was working with the therapist leading the group on a dream she had the night before. In the dream, a man in the dark is sneaking up on her and is trying to kill her with a knife. While playing the part of the man in the dark, she realized that he reminded her of her father. She and the therapist continued by working in the area of her fear of her father, his sneaking into her room when she was a child, and his ambition for her to become successful.

On my way home that night, I remembered that the therapist had gotten sidetracked and forgotten that the man in the dark was a part of the dreamer, and that the woman was projecting in her dream that she was trying to kill herself, or at least a part of her was. Of course when I say I'm trying to kill myself, I mean I'm working too hard. This woman, at the time of the dream, may have been working too hard or doing too much. Of course, her father may have been trying to get her to work harder. I don't know what was going on with her at that time. I can only project myself onto her dream. I do know that within six weeks of having that dream, she attempted suicide with an overdose of sleeping pills.

Fritz Perls warned against working on dreams that contain no life. I interpreted this to indicate Perls's belief that the dreamer did not feel like being alive.

As I have indicated in a previous chapter, I disagree with Perls that all the parts of the dream are unacceptable (disowned) parts of the dreamer. My dreams contain both acceptable (owned) parts as well as unacceptable (disowned) parts. This is one of only a few areas in which I disagree with Perls. However, I owe much to his work.

17
Dream Therapy in Groups

I have taken part in many dream groups as a participant. In these groups, one person worked alone with the leader while as many as forty sat silently observing. I agree that this was extremely therapeutic for that one person, but what about the other participants? Observing may be of some value, but I get extremely bored.

My interest did pick up when I started leading dream groups. However, I was concerned about the other participants being bored while I worked with one person. On one occasion I turned around and half the group had left.

At this point, I decided that I wanted to find a technique or way of working with dreams that is interesting and more therapeutic for the observers. I found that this can be done by involving all of the participants and having them act out the dream by becoming the different parts. It's my conclusion that this may be less therapeutic for the dreamer, but more therapeutic for the others.

This can be done in many ways. The following is the

structure I am using now. I intend to improve this with experience. Do not take this to be "the method." Change it to fit your own style and situation.

1. First the dreamer tells the dream in first person, present tense. This is done to re-experience the dream in the "here and now."
2. The second step is what Fritz Perls refers to as "setting the stage." The dreamer points out where each part is and where the action takes place. The room becomes the stage for the environment of the dream.
3. Group participants volunteer to play the parts of the dream. Each person chooses what part he or she wants to play within the parts available. If there are too few parts or too few people, one person can play several parts or several people can play the same part. If there are more parts than people, it is a good idea to have the dreamer play the spare parts Also, if I think a certain part would be good for the dreamer to play, I offer this idea for the dreamer's consideration.
4. Make it very clear to every participant that they are working with this dream as though this dream was their own dream. They are doing this for themselves and not for the original dreamer. However, this does not mean that the dreamer will not get value from the projections of others.
5. Act out the dream to give the participants a feel for their part.
6. One at a time, each person acts out their part, becoming that part, doing what that part did in the

dream, and talking about themselves as that part. Make sure they say how they feel as that part.
7. Have an encounter group, staying in role as each part of the dream, interacting with all the other parts.
8. Act out the dream and check how the dreamer is feeling.
9. Questions: questions can vary according to beliefs, experience, and where the group is. One question is enough, more than one is your choice. Here are a few suggestions; you create your own. The first one is my preference. You may use it if you do not have one of your own.
   A. What was the purpose of your choosing to create this dream?
   B. What is the purpose of this dream?
   C. What is the existential message you got from this dream? I prefer that the dreamer answer the first, and then anyone else who is willing answers the question prefixed with, "If I had created this dream . . ." or "If this were my dream . . ."
10. The dreamer is asked to change the dream to the way he or she wants the dream to be the next time. This is most useful for recurring dreams. About half refuse to change the dream, saying that it is already exactly the way they want it.
11. If the dreamer makes a change, we go through steps 1 to 10 again. The dreamer tells the new dream in first person, present tense.
12. The dreamer "sets the stage" for the changes.
13. Participants volunteer to play all the changes if there is only a slight change.

14. Act out the new dream.
15. Each new part talks about itself.
16. Have an encounter group.
17. Act out the dream and check how the dreamer is feeling.
18. Questions: What was the purpose of your choosing to create this new dream?

I feel very positive about this group approach for many reasons:
1. So far, every dreamer has either said so or has appeared, to me, to feel more positively, following this style of dream group experience, than before the group.
2. There is group participation with a safe structure in which each participant is talking about him or herself instead of talking about someone else.
3. For people new to groups, it is easier to play a part of someone else's dream and talk about themselves as that part, than it is to talk about themselves. They don't realize they are actually talking about themselves until they are really into it.
4. The participants are all very active and the leader becomes a participant who happens to know the structure.
5. There is an opportunity for participants to discover something about themselves.
6. The parts the participants play are their own choices. What they say and do as those parts is what the participants choose to do.

7. Each participant is working with the dream as though it is his or her own dream.
8. Participants are shown that they don't need an analyst to tell them about their dreams. They can work with their dreams alone, free of charge.
9. Participants are shown that they are the creators of their own dreams. They are responsible and create their dreams the way they want them.

The following is an example of how to use dreams with a group using this style. It was taped at the Freeman Institute in Santa Monica, California. The group was advertised in newspapers as a "Dream Group," with an entry fee of six dollars per person. This entire recording was transcribed exactly as recorded (Atwell 1980). No words were left out. The " . . . " indicates silence on the recording. This was a two-hour recording.

Leader: "I'd like a volunteer to tell us a dream and allow the entire group to work with that dream."

R: "I have a dream."

Leader: "Tell the dream as though the dream is happening right now, first person, present tense."

R: "OK, I hear the words 'key ring.' Just the words 'key ring,' and then I wake up and I think, 'key ring, what's that?' I go back to sleep and I dream that I'm riding down the elevator with my psychiatrist after a session. We get to the bottom of the elevator and I wonder what's going to happen now. I look at him and he's hurrying off and he's not saying good-bye to me. I feel a little put out . . . and I see that he gets into a white car and drives off. I look behind me, off to the corner, to see if my car is there and it is. Then I sit on a bench. I'm sitting on the bench and I find that I have his keys on a key ring. I have his keys . . . and yet he managed to get into his car, so I look at the key ring, and . . . I'm looking at the key ring and there are three regular keys on it and the rest of them are plastic keys, sort of potential, and I feel these are potential keys. These can be used if he wants to use them. I see they're kind of like a child's plastic keys. There is a long needle-like thing that's not really a key and I put that into the elevator slot and it opens, and I say, 'It opens!' and I think, 'Well, I'll leave them with the secretary,' but somehow, I don't actually do that. I pin the whole key ring thing, I pin it onto a book that I'm reading called *Feelings*. I pin it onto the page there. It seems that I'm wearing some kind of a badge and a woman comes up to me and I recognize her. She's a woman who used to be . . . I see that she is a merchandising educator with Thrifty Drug. She recognizes me, but she's in a different context, because we're not in the drugstore business. I'm sitting here, and she comes up to me and says, 'Do you go to conferences?' and I say, 'Yes, I've been to four lately.' So she says, 'Well, I'll get you a badge of your own.' I feel humble because I feel, 'Maybe this is my psychiatrist's badge.' I'm confused: 'His badge! . . . and I have his keys . . . and I have his keys . . . and she's going to issue me a badge, or something,' and then she gives me a dress and I say, 'I would have gone to Elysium, but it's my birthday.' . . . And so, she doesn't give me a badge, but she gives me a dress and it's green and it's kind of chiffon. It has several parts, like a whole robe . . . And it has little squares on it. So, I take this from her . . . And that's it."

Leader: "OK, I'd like to use this dream because it seems to have so much happening in it and so many different objects. Quite often when people tell a dream, there are just a couple of things they mention and it's not enough to work with. This dream has a lot of things to work with, and probably more than we'll have time to work with tonight. The next step would be for you to do what Fritz Perls called, 'setting the stage.' Use this room as the environment of the dream. Point out where each thing is, where the action is taking place, so that we can act out this dream, using this room as the stage. Where would you like the elevator to be in this room? . . . And so forth."

R: "The elevator is here. My shrink went off in his car . . . Where she is sitting. My car is where the tape recorder is . . . I'm sitting on a bench here, slightly in front of, and to the side of the elevator. The woman educator comes to me from there . . . And I know that if I take the key ring to the secretary, it's one floor up. I guess I have that in my mind."

Leader: "The keys, I thought, were very important for a number of reasons. So, I would like you to play the part of the keys. You can also play the part of yourself in this dream, since you're the one who's having the dream. For the rest of the parts, I would like the group members to volunteer and choose a part of her dream to play, and act out this dream. One part, I think would be enough, and if we don't use all the parts, it's not necessary. I think I'll play your car."

J: "I'll play your psychiatrist."

M: "I could be the merchandise woman, or whatever."

H: "I could be the elevator."

R: "What else is there? . . . A dress . . ."

B: "The dress."

Leader: "And a book of feelings, also . . ."

R: "Oh yes, there's a book . . . a book of feelings."

Leader: "Is that everyone? Does everyone have a part?"

O: "I don't have a part."

M: "There's the bench."

Leader: "What would you like? Is there anything in the dream that you remember that you'd be willing to act out?"

O: "The psychiatrist's white car."

D: "I'm the bench."

R: "I don't have a dress yet."

D: "You don't have a dress yet? . . . All right, I'll be the dress."

R: "I guess I was casting you as the dress."

D: "OK, I'll be the dress."

Leader: "You could do both parts, also."

D: "The dress and the bench? . . . all right."

Leader: "We've all got a part? OK, just so that we get a feel of our part, I'd like to go through the dream with each of us playing the part and taking the position of that part, like the elevator standing where the elevator is . . . the cars acting like cars and sitting in a car position."

H: "I'll have to make a choice though, whether to play the shaft or the cabin of the elevator. I don't want to play both."

Leader: "So we'll take our positions and walk through the

dream. Tell us what's happening again like you did, as though it's happening right now."

R to the elevator: "How are (J) and I going to get in you?"

Leader: "Well, he can hold his arms out around you, like this."

R: "That's right, yeah."

Leader: "Get in there and . . . "

J: "What was (B's) part? I forgot."

B: "I'm an open book."

J: "Oh!"

B: "I think I'd better be closed! I'm not going to be able to do that for the next hour!"

H: "That was good, though . . . Leave it open till you get tired."

R: "OK. So, let's go through it."

J to R referring to the elevator: "Punch his button."

R: "We're in the elevator and we're going down the elevator and we get out . . . I'm a little unsure what's going to happen, and you don't acknowledge me by saying good-bye . . . And I look at my car and I see it's there. Oh, I've got to get my book . . . and I sit on the bench . . ."

B: "Oh, I shouldn't be here."

R: "I guess I have to pick you up or something."

B: "Good luck!"

R: "Oh, I have his keys . . . And I take the needle key and I open the elevator door and I see that does it, and it opens . . . I'll read my book . . . So I won't forget I'm pinning my keys onto the book page of feelings . . . So I won't forget to return them . . . I'm going to return them up the elevator . . . And I'm talking to the merchandising educator. That's the educator . . . Comes up, mentions my badge and asks me . . ."

M as educator: "Have you gone to conferences?"

R correcting M: "Do you go to conferences?"

M as educator: "Do you go to conferences?"

R: "Yes, I've been to four."

M as educator: "Maybe I should give you a badge."

R correcting M: "I will give you a badge."

M as educator: "I will give you a badge."

R: "And then I look in my book and I say to you, 'I would have gone to Elysium, but it's my birthday.' I'm just sort of a little overwhelmed with it all. There are so many parts . . . I've got a three piece outfit and it's green with squares on it . . . You are green with squares on you and soft . . ."

Leader: "OK, in the next part, stay in your role as that part, do what that part does, and talk about yourself as that part. Become that part and talk about yourself. I'll be your car and do this first to give you some idea how it goes. O.K.? . . . . I'm (R's) car, and I'm parked over here . . . . . . I'm grey. I use a lot of gas. I've got a lot of things in me. I'm very busy and I go places. I seem to have so much to do. I'm not taken care of very well. I like (R) and I go places with her. I see many things. I've got a lot of miles on me and I'm getting very old or experienced. I think I'd like to be a different color . . . . Maybe I'd like to be red. I feel busy, tired, and worn out. I feel like I'd like to rest and that's what I'm doing. I am just parked here, resting."

D: "I want a couple of more details . . . . Could you tell me . . . . . . What tone of green am I?"

R: "It's bright green."

D: "Vivid?"

R: "A vivid green."

D: "Rich?"

R: "They're extremely green."

D: "O.K,. and the squares again are?"

R: "Prints . . . . . . sSquares."

D: "O.K., sort of geometric?"

R: "Yeah, they're small."

D: "Are they small, or kind of medium-sized?"

R: "They're about so big."

D: "O.K., that's enough."

Leader: "I'd like to clarify one thing . . . . . . We are forgetting that this is (R's) dream and consider it to be a dream of our own. I'm doing this as though I dreamed this dream. So if I want to change it or elaborate on it, or if the dress is a different color, that's OK. Whatever I say is OK because it's my dream that I'm working on."

B: "Thank you for making that clear. I didn't understand that."

D: "I . . . OK, that doesn't make sense to me, but I will pass on that. If it's for her enlightenment, then I will go along."

Leader: "We're each in this for our own enlightenment, and we're not doing anything for (R), we're doing this for ourselves."

D: "OK."

B: "I'm a book called *Feelings*. There are a lot of books like me around, you know. Everybody's into writing some kind of a book that will sell, that's popular on the market. There's another book called *Caring*, and *Be the Person You Were Meant to Be*, and you name it, and there's a book out. I'm into *Feelings* and it's really a good book for me to be because I'm into 'feelings,' too. I'm hearing by the tone of my voice that I'm not feeling . . . proud, like I'm not a really fine piece of literature. Some people read me and get something out of me and maybe it's something they've read before, and they're just hearing it in a slightly different way, and a lot goes on and they say, 'Oh, I like that.' So, I sell a lot of copies. I'm not really clear why (R) is reading me now because she's so . . . so educated and so sophisticated and so literate and so profound . . . Maybe someone lent me to her, or gave me to her. I'm just not sure about that, but I'm really glad to be going around with her; its better than laying on a shelf someplace. So here I am . . . waiting, while she's reading . . . and I really didn't like that she stuck that weird, needle-shaped key into me. That hurt and I thought she wasn't being sensitive to my needs. I guess maybe she sees me as being an inanimate object, but I have feelings too! . . . Period."

J: "I'm (R's) psychiatrist. I have a lot on my mind today and I didn't feel I did very well in (R's) session. I think the reason she comes to me is because I take her MediCal stickers. I'm in a hurry to get going; I've got to get gas for my car . . . Got to . . . drive up and park it and walk across the rock slide and sit on an RTD bus for another half an hour . . . A pain in the neck. I've been doing this a while. I'm a little burned out; I'm not as enthusiastic as I used to be. I hide behind my degree quite a bit and I like it there . . . That's it . . . "

M: "I'm . . . the merchandising educator. I like seeing (R) . . . It reminds me of another time when I went to a conference with her and I kind of miss not seeing her at conferences. I'd like the opportunity to validate her. That's why I'd like to give her a badge. I feel a little envious of her . . . Looking at what she's been doing with her life, and me in my dull job. I'd like to go to conferences in my free time. I'd like to see more of (R), too. I just feel kind of bored with my life. I wish there were a lot more going on. (R) looks real pretty and free. I'm so envious. I'd like to be like her."

O: "OK. I'm (the psychiatrist's) car. I'm sleek and shiny white. Very well waxed and polished and cleaned. I have wide black wall 60 series tires with white lettering on them. Racing type . . . big, beefy treads and highly polished MAG wheels. I'm always kept very well vacuumed and cleaned on the interior. All the theater seats are clean, supple and smooth. I'm not worried about the gas crunch because I get great mileage, too. I feel like I'm well taken care of. I'm able to take care of myself and give something back to my driver, who seems to express a certain amount of pride in keeping me up, and likes being seen in me because I do something for his image, too. Sigh!"

D: "Is that the end?"

O: "That's the end . . . That satisfied sigh was the end."

D: "Well . . . I'm (R's) dress . . . And the nice educator gave me to her. I think that was really nice, because I think (R) would appreciate some excitement in her life and I'm obviously the kind of thing that you would wear to something that was really kind of special. Maybe, to a concert. In fact, that's exactly where I think I would want to go . . . a concert. I'm a little . . . frilly, but that's OK, because I deserve to be worn as often as possible and there are only so many things people around here dress for these days. I concede I'm not the very latest style, because I'm awfully layered . . . But then it's nice to be standing out a little bit. I love my color, or I should say I have a slight ambivalence about it . . . but vivid green is a perfectly outrageous color and it will let (R) express that side of her. And if some people think it's slightly garish, well that's just tough . . . because everybody's going to notice her, and it will make her feel very feminine in a more traditional sense, and that's OK . . . a lot of us have been robbing ourselves of that lately. All in all, I think she was rather surprised to receive me as a present, but I think it's very nice. I think we will blend together very nicely.

H: I'm an elevator. I have no idea how many story building I'm in, but sure that everybody who rides me knows."

R: "It's two."

H: "I'm apparently an elevator in a two-story building, and I'm reminded of a great uncle of mine who was an elevator in a county library. One of the most amusing things that happened to me in my life was hearing my great uncle talk about the people he would carry up and down to the third floor. One woman, who was a driver of the elevator, who was reading books on the elevator, was especially instructing. But I digress. I'm an old enough elevator now that I'm entitled to take a rest occasionally. I enjoy the work . . . going up and down, up and down, the conversation especially . . . I'm even put to mind of an occasion where still another friend of ours . . . a friendly contemporary elevator had some people making out in it . . . thinking they were unobserved, but actually they could be seen by the elevator . . . I saw the whole thing. At any rate, I have a great imagination. I wouldn't have to see it. I like being in motion when I feel like it, and resting the rest of the time. Fortunately, my need for rest is enough so that a few busy times during the day don't wear me out. I hope that I can be a symbol for (R) of the fact that life has its ups and downs."

R: "I'm the keys. I'm (R's psychiatrist's) keys and (R) has landed with me . . . I'm landed with (R) and so I'm here, but I don't know why. There are several of me, you know. First, I'm the needle-like one that would hook on the end, and I notice that she has managed to open up the elevator with me, and I must say I'm a funny-looking key . . . For a key, I look very different from any other key. Well . . . if it's not boasting, I've never seen another one like me. I wonder where my relatives are. The only relative I can think of . . . closest-looking to, so probably related to me, is a key that goes into a cash register at Thrifty Drug Store, but I'm even funnier than that key . . . and . . . further on down from me here . . . We have the metal keys. One of them looks sort of short and one of them looks long. The short one looks sort of . . . it could be a car key, and . . . oh, I could be a car key. I could be a house key; I'm bigger . . . All those little ones could become keys with time . . . We're plastic keys . . . and we're on the way. Oh, what's happening now? Well, now we're getting . . . pinned into this book. (B as the book makes a squealing noise) Since we're educated keys, we can see that the book is called *Feelings*. Oh, I'm the sharpest key, so I can hear a little squeak coming out of the page. Now that we're pinned to it, I don't know why the hell we haven't been taken up the elevator to wait on the secretary's desk. I suppose it's more exciting having this time here. I guess it's pretty damned exciting, actually. It's kind of insecure, because what's she going to do with us? . . . All this business about pinning us, so that she'll remember . . . It strikes me that she doesn't really want to remember to return us, and that's why she's going to such great lengths, to mention it. She's got us pinned to *Feelings*. Well, I'm pretty needle-like myself. I'm the smartest, sharpest key and I guess I'll . . . That's it, now it seems I'm going to be upstaged by a dress. Oh, and there's something else pinning on here . . . I see it's a badge thing . . . Oh! Nobody?"

J: "It would be interesting for you to be the badge."

R: "Yeah! . . . OK. I'm a badge and it's a little bit embarrassing because . . . but, (R) is . . . I'm embarrassing to (R) because she didn't notice she was wearing me . . . She's confused . . . God, that woman gets confused often . . . I mean, how can you be confused when you're wearing me . . . a badge! I mean, a badge is an unconfuser . . . deconfuser! There's this other woman coming up now! She's going to replace me with another badge . . . Oh, I see . . . I'm not really (R's) badge. Well, I'm feeling insecure, because I don't know whose badge I am, or why I'm stuck on her shoulder. I don't know what's going on here, I don't understand it! I mean, a badge is a definite item; I'm a definite item, and I know I should have a definite place . . . She's not awfully keen on badges. She feels embarrassed that she's wearing me. She doesn't know why she's wearing me and why. I'm not hers, and she's not anxious to wear badges at all! How can anybody be so stupid? . . . I mean it's very distinctive to wear me . . . Or any of my cousins, sisters, or aunts. So . . . I'll have to see what fate brings . . ."

Leader: "OK, what I'd like for us to do now, is to fantasize that we came to an encounter group, each as the part that we played in the dream. And we're going to sit here and talk with each other and interact with each other as an encounter group of dream parts."

B: "I love it!"

Leader as (R's) car: "For instance, I like keys very much, because they get me started every morning, and I can't do anything until I see keys. So I feel very close to you."

B as book: "I feel annoyance. I mean, you opened the elevator to take the keys upstairs, which was the only logical, reasonable, rational thing to do! And then like some kind of a nut, you came back and jabbed yourself into me! And what . . . I've got to wear you until you see that nut again? Whenever that's going to be . . . A week, or a half a week, or whatever? I've got to walk around with something coming through my . . . left shoulder?"

J as psychiatrist: "I'm very unconcerned about you, keys, because I have another pair, which I used to drive away in my car with, so I don't think I'll need you until I get back to my . . ."

D as dress: "(O), what kind of car were you? I know you wear MAG wheels and all that, but . . ."

O as psychiatrist's car: "Well, I'm either a Mazda RX 7 or a . . . I don't feel like a Porsche, I feel like a Japanese make . . ."

D as dress: "Well, do you feel like a Datsun 280? (B laughs) Well, I need to know!"

O as psychiatrist's car: "It's not a Honda. I'd rather be a Mazda RX7 . . . it just came out . . . "

D as dress: "Oh, a Mazda, well . . . that's the one with big tread. Oh, I have to talk as the dress . . . Well, I just think I'd look really spiffy in you and I just . . . you would . . . I wish I didn't get so turned on by things like you, but I do. I just can't help it. And . . . I mean, at least I'm high class, so I belong in . . . I'll take your word that you're a good-looking Mazda."

B as book: "I don't have many feelings about cars."

H as elevator: "I'd like to graduate into a building that is at least three stories high. It's really very limiting."

R as keys: "You've got a basement."

H as elevator: "Oh, I get to go to the basement? But only occasionally."

R as keys: "That's where the cars are."

H as elevator: "Oh, yeah . . . Well, I'm really very pleased to learn that. You see, I didn't have a brain until now."

R as keys: "As a key, I must have had a microcomputer

attached to me, that I injected there . . . Slipped myself into you there."

H as elevator: "I had no problem with your opening me up like that. I was pleased and hoped you'd just stay longer."

B as book: "I wish you'd lend me to your psychiatrist. (to J) It seems to me that you could use something about feelings."

J as psychiatrist: "She knows I don't approve of these pop books, anyway."

R as keys: "Well , as a key, I feel like . . . I feel the need to be facilitative between you two. I feel that the psychiatrist didn't talk directly to the book."

J as psychiatrist: "No, I'm talking directly to (R), I believe . . ."

B as book: "I understood the leader just said that we should have an encounter between the parts."

J as psychiatrist: "Oh!"

B as book: "I felt dismissed when you said, 'I'm not into pop books.' . . . I mean, it's OK for me to say that . . . maybe I'm not one of the ten greatest books of the century, but for you to dismiss me like that . . . I feel really wiped out."

J as psychiatrist: "Sort of erased, huh?"

B as book: "Very funny!"

H as elevator: "Don't forget that 'pop' means popular."

B as book: "I didn't ask for any help from you."

H as elevator: "That's helpful?"

B as book: "I didn't ask for any hindrance from you! (to J) I'd like you to say something directly to me.

J as psychiatrist: I wish that you would quit being around (R) so she wouldn't have time to read you."

B as book: "Why don't you tell her not to read me: I'm sure she would listen to you."

H as elevator: "She's not even here."

J as psychiatrist: "She's not here?"

H as elevator: "How can we talk to her?"

J as psychiatrist to B: "You can just write it in one of your pages and she'll get to you soon."

H as elevator: "I wonder why she didn't come here, since this whole thing concerns her dream. Couldn't we send for her?"

D as dress: "She's bathing, gang, until she can get me on, if you don't mind."

H as elevator: "You mean bathing is going to make it easier?"

B as book: "This is like a part where she just observes."

J as psychiatrist: "Slither in."

B as book: "Slither into it while she's wet. You can imagine what that'll do for chiffon."

M as educator: "I feel left out. Kind of withdrawn, I guess. I guess that's why I want to give you . . . as a gift . . . a dress, because then maybe I'll be liked, and accepted a little more for who I am. I'm kind of shy, and I kind of hide behind the cash register just kind of . . . I see people a little bit, but I'm kind of afraid of people and sort of back off. But I really would like to get closer to people."

B as book: "Well, you could be close to me anytime."

H as elevator: "You could be close to me anytime."

M as educator: "OK."

H as elevator: "We could go for rides together."

M as educator: "Oh God, I really . . . "

J as psychiatrist to M: "I have an appointment open for you next week."

B as book: "That's ambulance chasing!"

R as keys: "I've got one or two pals here on this key ring . . . we like to go out for a spin . . . I mean, we keep getting into a lot of holes. We like a change of place, a change of scene, and here we are . . . pinned to . . . *Feelings* here doesn't appreciate us one bit . . . *Feelings!*"

B as book: "Well, what would you expect, *Feelings!* Not to feel?"

R as keys: "You're labeled "feelings," but my feelings are hurt, because I think I'm a pretty damned sharp cookie here and I . . ."

B as book: "You are sharp! That's what . . . it was your sharpness that hurt me!"

R as keys: "I want you to feel honored for them hanging on you."

B as book: "Oh, Jesus Christ . . . You should excuse the expression!"

H as elevator: "Superstar?"

B as book: "I should feel honored that you stuck the nails in me!"

R as keys: "Well, . . . I'm restless. I mean (my psychiatrist) is sort of a dull fellow anyway . . . but now . . . now, here . . . What the hell . . . I mean . . . OK, I got a little thrill getting into the el—yeah, getting into, you know, the little hole there, but . . ."

H as elevator: "How about hiding at the bottom of the basement? And let him look for you. Just give him a hint."

J as psychiatrist: "Key ring . . . I want to tell you this . . . You could be more complete by adding keys onto you that I need that you don't have. You would have a much happier life . . . You would become my principle key ring instead of my secondary key ring."

R as keys: "Well, listen!"

J as psychiatrist: "If you took those baby keys off of you . . ."

R as keys: "Let's forget that . . . OK . . . So she didn't get me back up so that I'd get back to you . . . Maybe I'll stay with her . . . I mean, OK, this is her book, *Feelings*. . . Well, she's been carrying the book. I'll see what happens . . . Let's see, I'll stay with her and she'll take me to . . . I mean, I'll stay with *Feelings* here . . . Sorry I'm not too fond of you, but that's the kind of book you are . . ."

B as book: "It looks so nice to walk around carrying a book."

R as keys: "You're a nice solid hardback, I'll tell you that, but here I'm pinned to one of your pages. And if you wouldn't complain about it, I would have been happy, but I feel slighted . . . Anyway, I'm stuck to you . . . but look at all the other fellows here . . . There's glad rags here . . . I've already met elevator, but look at this . . . This fancy car has roared off . . .

Oh no, has roared back here . . . and I must have been in . . . I've never been in that kind of dumpy old gold car. You never know, it might be something interesting. Maybe I'll pin myself . . . Maybe I'll throw myself onto Miss Doll's hands here and she'll take me around the various Thrifty Drugs."

M as educator: "Do you like that?"

R as keys: "I'm having an identity crisis."

B as book: "What a lofty ambition."

M as educator: "You could be my friend."

R as keys: "Oh hell, lady, why don't you go to Elysium instead of Thrifty Drug?"

M as educator: "I can't . . . It's your birthday."

H as elevator: "Birthday suit?"

B as keys: "I wonder what (R) meant by that? She would have gone to Elysium except for the fact that it was her birthday."

R as keys: "Are you trying to graduate to a second-rate book?"

B as book: "Graduate to a second-rate book . . . Oh boy . . . insults and injuries."

J as psychiatrist: "Is that getting into the Freudian credits? I believe . . ."

B as book: "No, I really would like to know what she meant. I wonder if you guys have any idea."

H as elevator: "What?"

D as dress: "She just got me . . ."

B as book: "She would have gone to Elysium today, except that it's her birthday.

H as elevator: "Oh!"

R as keys: "Well, you know what I heard? Because I pick up all sorts of stuff . . . I heard that you were given to her for her birthday . . . but if you look on the last page there you . . ."

B as book: "Is there something on the last page? When was her birthday?"

R as keys: "Well, it says the date right there . . . It says April sixth?"

B as book: "April sixth?"

H as elevator: "It's very hard for a book to read itself . . . Really asking for a lot."

B as book: "She had a birthday on April sixth and didn't tell her training group about it?"

R as keys: "How the hell do you know about her training group? You must be . . . "

B as book: "She's been carrying me around for a while now, and I listen . . . I really take in. I'm a sponge . . . That's one of my problems."

R as keys: "I'll have to loosen up on you. Instead of sticking to you, I'll have to wait around you."

B as book: "Ah, that's nice . . . I like that."

Leader: "OK. I'd like to close this encounter group. It's always hard for me to find a place to do that, and I think this is about it. So, I'd like us to run through the dream one more time, with you going through it again, and keeping us informed of what's happening with you as you go through the dream."

R: "What's happing with me as me?"

Leader: "As you, yes."

H: "Only time I've ever been an elevator."

J: "I'm sure you've had other uplifting experiences."

H: "How did you enjoy being a psychiatrist?"

J: "I let my negative side come out."

R: "I'll be happy to have you cancel my outstanding bill . . . Being so high . . . Since you think that the only reason I come to you is for the insurance."

J: "I have unpaid accounts all the time; it's just a tax deduction."

R: "Oh great, thanks for permission!"

J: "One of the reasons I charge such a high fee, it evens out . . . "

R: "Well, thanks for taking my insurance . . . for partial coverage."

B: "What are we up to now? I thought (R) was going to go through the dream again."

Leader: "Yes, we're just waiting for (D) to come back from the restroom."

B: "Oh, for (D)."

Leader: "Well, I guess we could start without her because her part is at the end of the dream. OK, let's go through it again with each one of us in our place. The elevator where the elevator is, and act it out again."

H: "Places!"

J: (to R) "Aren't you supposed to be saying something?"

R: "Oh! . . . Well, we could say something . . . Oh, are we supposed to say something? I thought . . . Oh, this time I'm supposed to say something?"

Leader: "Just keep us informed of what's happening with you as we go through the dream."

R: "OK . . . (My psychiatrist) is rushing off into (his car) right now . . . And I'm glancing off at my car and . . . my car . . . You're kind of off to the side . . . I'm just reassured that you're there . . . And I'm sitting on the bench, and I open my book. I'll open my book. Is this just supposed to sketch it, that's all? Or I say something about what's happening?"

Leader: "You can say how you're feeling or whatever . . . "

R: "Well, I'm feeling that maybe there's more to this book than I . . . It's an impressive-looking book. I don't know, though . . . And my former Thrifty merchandising educator seems to be approaching me. Oh, I left out the keys! God, I left out the key thing, the keys. Didn't mention the keys. Got to the book without mentioning the keys. I didn't do that, but now I remember it. Oh, like I found the keys, and then I try the elevator, and it opens, and then I'm wondering . . . What shall I do? I have my book and I . . . Oh, I'll pin the keys to the book, so I won't forget. Pin the keys to the feelings. (B as book makes a squealing noise) Oh, what's she doing here, I wonder? Oh, she's the educator."

M as educator: "Have you been to any conferences?"

R: "I've been to four."

M as educator: "I was looking for a badge . . . I want to give you one . . . It's your birthday."

R: "Well, I would have been to Elysium today, only it's my birthday."

M as educator: "Oh, well look what I have for your birthday."

R: "Hmmm . . . Kind of square, but . . . She's aluminous . . . These dresses that answer back! Good looking, but kind of square. Very graceful. Why the hell did that somebody knock at the door and wake me up out of this dream, because I was dreaming and . . . I was awakened . . . Thank you . . . "

Leader: "Now I'm going to ask you a couple of questions, and after you've answered, anybody in the group who wants to, can answer the question as though the dream is your dream, OK? And you're answering for yourself. All right, the first question I'm going to ask you is: What was the purpose of your creating this dream?"

R: "The purpose of my creating this dream was to find out what I meant by "key ring," because I heard the words "key ring" in the dream just before I woke up to go to the bathroom."

Leader: "Did you find that out?"

R: "I'm not sure. I certainly found out a lot. I certainly experienced a lot. I just hadn't experienced it before."

Leader: "OK. Would anyone else like to answer that question? What would be the purpose of your creating this dream if you had this dream?"

B: "The purpose of the dream for me is to allow me to know something of my many values."

D: "The purpose of my dream is to let me know that maybe I need to be moving on, and not seeing my psychiatrist anymore. He's given me the keys that he has to give me. I have my book. I have created pretty new dresses."

J: "Maybe I had a rebirthing, so it's my birthday."

H: (to D) "I like yours. I'll buy that."

Leader: "I like that, too. Anybody else?"

M: "I think I might have created this dream to show me how I grow, and how I have a lot more growing to do, because the keys have some little baby parts that can become wiser and more experienced . . . And I'm pretty pleased with myself, being the needle key. I'm sure of myself. I can open up some doors on my own and I'm being more independent and in control of my life."

H: "I had some hesitations about terminating, because I owe him so much money. This is a minor supplement."

R: "Oh, I keep getting you mixed up with the elevator . . . I'm sorry. I was wondering why the elevator was in debt."

J: "I was wondering why the elevator was in therapy."

R: "It wants to go sideways, what else."

B: "Maladjustment . . . It doesn't accept reality . . . It wants to be in a three story building."

H: "Tired of the same old shafting."

M: "I think another reason I might have created this dream

is to look at how I sometimes get confused about who I am, what my identity is . . . and . . . Other times, I'm real sure about who I am, what I'm doing and . . . But then there are times when I really don't know."

Leader: "I was thinking that possibly the purpose of my creating this dream was to realize that I'm tired of the car that I have and that I'm jealous of people who have fancy cars, and I'd really like to have a new car."

R: "I think the reason that I dreamt that I . . . Oh, I feel that I dreamt this dream to show myself the needle key, seeing as how in an earlier dream that night, I dreamt that I was buying needles and thread in Thrifty Drug store . . . for 29 cents. Oh, I'm so mundane . . . No, I think that one of the reasons that I created this dream was to really show this thick-head, who I can be sometimes, some sharpness that's there . . . That needle in her earlier dream, and then another, earlier dream said "key ring," and then I put the needle on the key ring . . . and so . . . so . . . And I'm trying to sew things together . . ."

M: "The needle can't get to the point!"

B: "Nonsense! It's penis envy."

R: "I'll get to the point."

M: "So what?"

R: "Well, in her waking life, she beats around the bush a hell of a lot . . . Yes, that's why she's got a bushy dress, too."

Leader: "OK. I'd like to ask you another question. And that is, what would you like to change about this dream?"

R: "As a dream?"

Leader: "What would you like to be different?"

R: "OK. I would like the interaction between (my psychiatrist) and myself to be different. I wasn't satisfied. I felt slighted by him, and I'd like that to be different. And I would like the keys and the needle key, I would like them to be . . . to really . . . I would like them to show themselves, not as symbols, but as feeling . . . as what they are."

Leader: "OK. I would like you to set this up, this new dream, and we'll act it out, exactly the way you want it. And you make the dialogue between you and your therapist, and play the part of the keys, and make this dream exactly the way you would like to dream it next time."

R: "Oh . . . OK . . . (my psychiatrist) is kind of scary for me, though. Just in the context of the dream. (To psychiatrist): I'm unsure what I want with you, but I know that that's not what I want, for you to just go off like that, so . . . I want to talk with you. It's not enough. And I . . . I'm feeling very cheated, because . . . well, I'm feeling one-sided. I felt that . . . I felt good about complimenting you on a jacket which I first didn't mention and I think I want something back. You said that I had become more livelier . . . yes, more lively in a couple of sessions, and I . . . OK, well I am, and I'm feeling exposed. I'm feeling like . . . And I also feel how one-sided and wooden you used to be in this situation, and it's not enough that you just run off. I want to . . . I don't feel finished."

Leader: "OK, let me clarify. You're wanting the new dream to have that conversation in it?"

R: "Oh, I see. I guess I was . . . Do I have to say what he says, too?"

Leader: "Yes, I'd like you to create the whole thing."

R: "Oh, OK."

Leader: "Have the elevator again, and you and the therapist come out, and you can create exactly the dialogue that you want between the two of you, and we'll go through that. Or whatever you want to happen between you and the therapist."

R: "Can I use my therapist?"

Leader: "Yes."

H: "I think you'd better be him, anyway (J is asleep)."

R: "Oh, I'd better be him."

H: "Yeah, he looks a little out of it, anyway."

R: "What can you expect from a burned-out man who hides behind his degree? . . . So what shall I . . . OK."

R as psychiatrist: "Well, (R), it seems that you want something from me."

R: "Yes, I do."

R as psychiatrist: "Well, you know . . . tell me what you want. What is it that you want?"

R: "Well, I would like to be your friend. I feel frustrated by this artificial situation. I feel that you're hidden . . . "

R as psychiatrist: "Oh, that's a good one: I'm hidden. The all-time hidden one. That's a good one."

R: "Well, you have a point there. I have a lot of hidden parts."

R as psychiatrist: "Well, you seem to have exposed a couple of them lately."

R: "I feel like being treated by you. Maybe we could go for a walk holding hands or some friendly thing like that, some real connection."

R as psychiatrist: "Acting out!"

R: "He wouldn't say that in real life. Well I'm imagining that you think that that is an acting-out situation. And I feel that you're being . . . Anyway, the hell with it. I feel very defensive, but I would like to be with you in a real-life situation outside of that room, where I feel very defensive."

R as psychiatrist: "All right we'll go out and walk around for an hour or so in Century City."

R: "OK, that's fine . . . "

Leader: "Is there anything else about the dream that you would like to change?"

R: "Yeah, the keys . . . I'm the keys, although I'm so sharp and efficient, I did one thing, I showed her one thing . . . And now I'm going to do all sorts of other things to show her more . . . or demonstrate . . . What can the keys do? I'm going to open different doors. Some of these doors are people . . . I don't know, I'm just keys and sometimes I'm useful and sometimes I'm mysterious . . . I don't know how to change it . . . I'm starting to cry . . . I'm feeling very frustrated about that part . . . "

Leader: "I don't know whether to go on or stay with you and the way you're feeling now."

R: (crying) "I feel sad now . . . I did leave out the keys when we went through the whole thing. I left out the whole, main thing . . . I think I just changed my perspective because I'm caught up in all the images and what fun it was and everything. It really was a lot of fun for me. I kind of liked the images I got. I liked the acting and all the people doing this, and then I snapped. What I feel somehow means something. I don't know what it means, but that key business . . . I want to make a clearer message to myself, and then I feel like crying. I think a part of it is that I don't feel that . . . I was just thinking of something that wasn't in the dream, that I was reading Liv Ullman's *Changes* and I felt very sad. That was last night. I felt very sad . . . (crying)"

B: "It hurts to change."

R: "(crying) I was alone on Saturday night . . . I used to be with . . . somebody on Saturday nights, although I was never really excited about being with him; I think I was aware of missing him. I think I was kind of aware of that . . . and I knew he had gone out with another woman. So that's a change . . . (crying) . . . About the key ring business, my daughter had given him one. Actually, I had taken her to Las Vegas last year, to a conference in November, and she bought him a little key ring with a gun on it, and he didn't use it. He hasn't been using it. The little gunshot caps . . . (crying) . . . I'm feeling long-winded . . . And I'm feeling salvation . . . Thank you."

Leader: (sensing by the tone of her voice that she is finished) "Rather than going on, I want to stop here and allow you to experience your feelings."

18
How to Use Dreams to Facilitate Counseling a Couple

When counseling a couple, dreams are used primarily to facilitate communication within the couple. This can be done is several ways (Calogeras 1977; Goldberg 1974; Nell 1975).

One way communication can be increased is by instructing the couple to share their dreams and to discuss them with each other before getting out of bed each morning. When one of them does not remember a dream, they are to make up a dream with both of them in it. When neither remembers a dream, they are to make up a dream together and discuss it. In this way, the couple increases the time they are talking together in bed and ends the jumping out of bed when the alarm rings to go off to work. I believe that allotting a time to talk will improve communication and that improving communication will improve relationships. According to

Meredith Sabini (1972), sharing dreams will add a new, often deeper dimension to relationships. The couple could also, at other times, work on their dreams together, similar to the way I described for using dreams with group or individual counseling. This creates a togetherness in working together on their own growth in addition to communicative value.

When I dream about a person I know who is acting a certain way, I can consider that act in four different ways:
1. A projection of myself or what I'm doing.
2. What I believe that person is like, or is doing which I am also like or am also doing.
3. The way I want that person to be or to act.
4. The way I want to be or want to act.

In counseling, all four of these can be fully examined in addition to using dreams in all the ways I have previously discussed. Working on dreams alone may be enough to sufficiently improve the relationship.

Sidney Jourard (1971) believed that most problems that couples have with each other are due to lack of disclosure. I see working with dreams as an excellent way for each mate to disclose to the other. By talking about their dreams, they are talking about themselves.

Of course, working with dreams is best done in a counseling session. The counselor can watch for avoidance and facilitate communication. The dream is basically used as a starting point in working with the couple, similar to the way I have previously described as a method I use in working with a group. After starting with a dream, the counselor can move the work in the direction indicated by the dream.

For instance, if in the husband's dream, he has sex with his secretary, we can move in that direction. This is done by suggesting that the husband say to his wife, "I want to have sex with my secretary." This is followed by a dialogue or even an argument. Arguments can improve relationships by clearing the air. Some couples have been known to end up in bed after an argument. This may even improve the couple's sex life.

19
How to Use Dreams to Facilitate Counseling Children

Children's dreams are simpler and more clearly express their wants and fears, which Freud believed to be due to their having fewer defenses in their personality structure (O'Nell 1976). Actually, children's dreams are less complicated than those of adults because their thinking is less developed. Their dreams seem similar to their thinking while awake.

Jersild (1947) studied American children ages five through twelve. His findings generally show that dream content reflects the increasing maturity on the part of the child. Topics that increased with age were related to amusement, embarrassment, guilt, height, falling, prestige, achievement, independence, and loss of a loved one (O'Nell 1976).

Reports of unpleasant dreams also increase with age while themes of magic decrease. At ages five to six, 62 percent expressed a desire to have further dream experiences, ages seven to eight, 49 percent; ages nine to ten, 40 percent; and ages eleven to twelve, 37 percent. This indicates that by age twelve, 63 percent want to stop having dream experiences (O'Nell 1976).

Children may have more awareness of dreaming because they have a higher percentage of stage 1 (REM) time. A premature infant spends as much as 80 percent of sleep in stage 1 (REM). As the child grows older, stage 1 (REM) decreases. In addition to this, children also sleep more than adults. While some of the increase may be due to sleeping longer, children still have more stage 1 (REM) sleep than adults sleeping the same length of time. Because of the increase, children have more awareness of dreaming.

Children usually begin talking about dreaming almost as soon as they can talk, usually in the second year of life. Freud discussed one of his daughters' dreams in *The Interpretation of Dreams* that she reported at nineteen months of age (O'Nell, 1976).

Calvin Hall (1972) found twice as much aggression in the content of children's dreams as in adults' dreams. He also found far more sex in adults' dreams but sex was not absent in children's dreams.

Van de Castle (1970) found that the percentage of animals in dreams declined with age. His study showed that the dream images of children age four were 61 percent animals compared with nine percent at age 16. He found that adults average 7.5 percent with animal content.

He also found that early-maturing students had the lowest percentage of animal images by grouping early-maturing, later-maturing, and late-maturing students within the same age and comparing their dreams. Early-maturing groups had far less animals, and the late-maturing groups the most. Of course, this is different for some cultures. For example, adult aborigines have about 50 percent animals (O'Nell 1976).

David Foulkes (1975, 1977) found that dream recall increases with age. He did a five-year longitudinal sleep laboratory study of children aged three to fourteen. In five years, stage 1 (REM) dream recall increased from 27 percent to 67 percent. NREM dream recall increased from 6 percent to 40 percent. He also found an increase in realism, and that the children's dreams closely correlated with their waking development (Foulkes 1977).

In another study by Foulkes (1968) with children age four to six, dream recall was obtained from 44 percent of awakenings. The children's dreams were generally realistic, related to their everyday life, and free of disturbing affect or impulse. The most frequent content was recreational.

Shraga Zim (1975) did a study to discover if there would be changes in the dreams of children, which correspond to the cognitive changes that occur during waking. Zim found "shifts from a passive observer to an active participant." He also found changes from images of objects and animals to the family and age mates.

Always think and talk positively about dreaming when talking to children, if for no other reason than to encourage them to continue remembering dreams. This is an important part of the Senoi approach, as discussed earlier.

Don't wait until taking a child to a counselor to talk about dreaming; start early, and regularly talk about dreaming.

A woman who heard that I lead dream groups came to ask me what to do about her daughter. She was worried about her daughter's dreaming. She believed her daughter was having "nightmares," and whenever she asked her what she was dreaming, the daughter refused to tell her. I asked her how often she told her daughter her own dreams and she replied that she never had, as far as she could recall.

Children tend to copy whatever their parents model. If parents talk about dreaming, children talk about dreaming. A good way for a parent, or counselor, to begin to talk to children about dreaming is to first tell the child a dream or two of their own (Wicklund 1976). If the child does not remember a dream, ask the child to "create" a dream. Dreams created while awake can work very well.

How the counseling continues depends on the maturity of the child and the style of the counselor. The counselor is basically looking for answers to questions like:

1. How is the child feeling?
2. What are the child's wishes and fears?
3. How are parents portrayed in the dream?
4. What does the child want?
5. Who is in the dream and what is their relationship to the child?
6. Is the child rewarding or punishing him or herself with the dream?
7. Would the child have preferred to change the dream in some way?

With younger children, the dream can become a game with both the counselor and child playing the roles of the

different animals and objects. While playing the game, the counselor can ask questions like:
1. What kind of lion are you?
2. Are you a happy lion or a sad lion?
3. What are you sad about, lion?
4. What would make you happier?
5. What kind of lion would you like to be?

Another useful method is to have the child draw the dream; this is followed by having the child tell you about the drawing.

The C. G. Jung Institute of Los Angeles has hundreds of miniatures of people, monsters, animals, etc. They have children pick out miniatures and place them in a sand box and talk about their dreams while illustrating them in the sand box. This seems to be an excellent way to hold the child's interest.

20
How to Use Dreams to Facilitate Counseling a Family

While counseling with the child alone can be very productive, working with the entire family is much better. Dreams are valuable indicators of family dynamics and sharing dreams adds a new, often deeper dimension to the family relationship (Sabini 1972). Although working on dreams with a counselor is preferable, a family can also work with their dreams alone. Parents first, followed by older children, with the youngest child last, is usually the best order, depending on time. Once the family is experienced at working with dreams, it is unnecessary to have any specific order.

Style can range from playing the roles of dream animals to working with the dream as I have described as a method for working with a group.

When working with a counselor, the dream can also be

used as a starting point, as I described with couples. In fact, when working with a family, everything I have mentioned can be applied.

Henry Beck (1977) considers dreams to be of special value in working with families who block communication or only appear to be cooperative. Working with dreams helps to open new possibilities of communication for the family (Beck 1977).

21
Dream Now

In Dufour's (1975) direct-reverie therapy, clients create dreams in the presence of a therapist. In this way the dreaming process can be directly observed and understood.

Another way this can be done is with hypnosis. The client is first put into a "state of hypnosis" and then given a hypnotic suggestion to "dream now." The client is then given time to dream. Next, the client is brought out of the "state of hypnosis" and asked to report the dream. This "hypnotic dream" is then worked with in whatever style the therapist chooses (Walker 1974).

The idea of working with a present dream is great. A present dream is a better picture of the dreamer than a past dream. People continually change from moment to moment and their dreams change accordingly. Dreams exist in a continuous relationship with the waking state and share a common experiential background (Gentil 1978; Hendricks 1975; Levenson 1974).

Hypnotists assume that the "hypnotic dream" is something

over and above waking fantasy and stress the unique role of the "trance" in producing "hypnotic dreams." However, research does not support this contention (Walker 1974). "Hypnotic dreams" seem to be related to and are best described as "directed fantasy" according to Priscilla Walker (Walker 1974).

I recently experienced a "hypnotic dream" or "directed fantasy." After a lengthy process of deep relaxation, I was given a suggestion to "dream now." I experienced what I consider to be a very vivid "fantasy trip." Possibly this is what is generally called hypnosis. Whatever label is used, I did create a very dream-like fantasy. Fantasies can be worked with in the same way as a dream. In addition to this, waking fantasies are very similar to dreams (Gordon 1953; Klinger 1971; Sarason 1944; Shulman 1973; Starker 1974; Starker 1976; Starker 1977).

A study by Steven Stalker (1974) concluded that, "dreaming and daydreaming are viewed as analogous or parallel rather than alternative or unrelated." Singer and Antrobus (1963) found that daydreaming and dreaming is very similar. In another study with fifty-five subjects, Steven Stalker (1977) concluded "dreams and daydreams appear to be highly interrelated aspects of the fantasy process, sharing important affective and structural components.

I believe that a systematic program working with waking fantasies could be developed that would teach people how to change their waking fantasies. Since there is a correlation between waking fantasies and dreaming, both their dreaming and waking behavior could be changed as a result. Of course, I also believe that the reverse can be done. Working with dreams can change waking fantasies. Starker and Hasenfeld (1976) have already confirmed that "Positive-Vivid daydreamers are less prone to nightmares than individuals of the other daydreaming styles."

I also believe that dreaming can be changed simply by teaching subjects about dreaming and that they create their dreams the way they want them, just as they do their waking fantasies. Even sleep cycles can be changed in this way.

Edward Shollar (1975) did a study in which he fully informed subjects about relevant past sleep and dream studies and how to read their own EEG recordings. Following two adaptation nights and four to five baseline nights, he told them to end their stage 1 (REM) periods after eight minutes. They were also told not to end stage 1 (REM) periods by waking up, but to stay asleep and end them by changing to NREM.

Three of the four subjects successfully showed a decrease in the length of their stage 1 (REM) periods. The fourth showed no difference. He also found that pre-sleep instructions find their way into dreams and trigger the instruction. Those subjects that successfully followed instruction also reported that they were able to control their dreams while dreaming (Shollar 1975).

This demonstrates that we are capable of far more control during sleep than previously believed. I didn't even believe the sleep cycle could be controlled until reading the Shollar study (1975). Now I am even more convinced than ever that people dream what they want to dream.

David Wallin (1977) agrees that "dreaming is a deliberate process of creation," and developed an eight-week intentional-dreaming training program. This program was essentially a distillation of the three-point Senoi approach: confront danger, approach pleasure, and achieve a positive outcome. In addition to this he also used some Gestalt role-playing, visualization, active imagination, and self-suggestion. Dreams were collected from eight subjects two weeks prior to and during the eight-week program. Analysis of these dreams revealed "substantial change" in the imagery of five of the eight subjects (Wallin 1977).

I consider this to be outstanding and I want to develop a training program myself, similar to this. I believe that learning to become a more creative dreamer could shorten therapy or could be a therapy in its own right.

22
Conslusion About Dreams

As an eclectic therapist, I prefer to include dreams in the "tool chest" I use in doing therapy. Using dreams for therapy can increase my information about the client's various states of awareness and fantasies. Using dreams for therapy can also increase the client's self-awareness. I see dreams as being extremely valuable for both therapy and self-therapy. I believe a person can work alone with only dreams, as I have described, and achieve enough self-awareness to be helpful in personal growth.

However, working with a therapist is better. Avoiding is hard to control without a therapist present. I have a preference for a combination of self-help and sessions with a therapist at intervals. However, most of us do not have the money for a therapist and self-therapy is all we have.

I now work with my dreams while driving. Of course this is not the optimal circumstance, but it is sufficient to eliminate freeway boredom. I simply select items one at a time from dreams and talk about myself as that item, first person, present tense. Of course, in order to do self-therapy of this style, dreams are handy but unnecessary. I can choose any item I see or create an imaginary one using visual imagery.

The best way to work with dreams for self-therapy is to work on the dream while dreaming. Often, while dreaming, I work on items, which I reject as not belonging to me until I own them. I do this by becoming the item and talking about myself as that item *during* the dream. For example, while dreaming, I was walking up a stairs and came to a book on the stairs. I asked, "What is this book doing here?" I picked it up and looked at it. The title was *Statistics*. I said, "This is not mine!" I decided to work on this book as part of my dream while dreaming because the book did not belong to me. I said, "I am a statistics book. I know a lot about statistics. That's true, I do know a lot about statistics. I have taken three statistics classes. This is a part of me." I tossed the book over my shoulder and I continued up the stairs.

In my view, there is little that is mysterious about dreaming. The mystery about dreaming was created by those who earlier tried to explain their fantasies about dreaming. By rejecting the unconscious model, dreaming is simply a continuation of waking.

Overall assessment based on experimental research is not yet possible, but my own view as a result of immersing myself in the literature of dreaming is that:

1. All stages of sleep are capable of dreaming. Kamiya (1962) concluded, "Dreams can occur outside of Rapid Eye Movement periods as well as during them."
2. The EEG is of little or no value when identifying dreaming. Giora and Elam (1974) summed up by

saying that, "EEG indices alone fail to identify mental activity during NREM sleep, and thus should be abandoned as the method of proving cortical arousal during sleep."
3. Dreaming is continuous throughout most, if not all, sleep. As Hervey de Saint-Denys (1982) wrote: "There is no sleep without dreams, just as there is no waking state without thought" (Garfield 1974).
4. Dreaming is a continuation of, and is compatible with, waking. Steven Starker (1977) concluded that: "Dreams and daydreams appear to be highly interrelated aspects of the fantasy process, sharing important affective and structural components."
5. Awareness does not stop during sleep. Steven Starker (1974) found: "The results of this study suggest that certain parameters of cognitive processes remain in effect despite transitions from wakefulness to sleep; that dreams and daydreams share common properties."
6. During sleep, people create their dreams exactly the way they want them. I agree with David Wallin (1977) that, "Dreaming is a <u>deliberate</u> process of creation."

I now believe that it is better to train people to be more creative in their deliberate dreaming than to work with the dream content. However, working with dream content will also enable people to become more creative in their dreaming.

23
Self-Therapy

Paying a professional listener a lot of money just to listen to you can be great. Much can be gained from doing that. Finding the best psychotherapist and paying a hundred dollars or more an hour for the best psychotherapy can even be fantastic.

However, most of us cannot afford to pay a hundred dollars an hour or even a sliding scale. Most important is the fact that a good therapist is very hard to find. I have participated in groups with many psychotherapists. I have found some of the best psychotherapists in the world. Eric Marcus, MD, co-founder of the Los Angeles Gestalt Institute, and Nathaniel Branden, PhD (1992), to name only two, are doing fantastic work and they are capable of anything. However, I cannot afford to pay them what they are worth. So, where can I find a psychotherapist that I can afford? Sometimes it is hard to see the most obvious.

I have found the best psychotherapist in the world for me and I see him every morning and I pay him what he is worth.

He is waiting for me every morning when I wake up and walk into the bathroom. He is that person staring me in the face in the bathroom mirror. I hardly recognize him anymore, because he is getting older. I often start by asking, "Who are you?"

I am convinced that the best therapist in the world for me is myself and the best therapist in the world for you is you. Yes, this is sort of like being your own lawyer. He who is his own therapist has a fool for a client. We only appreciate what we pay for. I have heard all this. I understand what you are saying. However, I am convinced that the best therapist I can find is myself.

Self-therapy has many great advantages:
1. There is no therapist who knows more about me than I know about myself.
2. Self-therapy is free.
3. My Self-therapist is always with me where ever I go. He is right there any time I need him.
4. No appointments are necessary.
5. My self-therapist observes everything I do, all of my behavior.
6. My self-therapist is very much like Carl Rogers (1980, 2003). He gives me unconditional positive regard and reflection.
7. My self-therapist tells me what I want to hear and what I don't want to hear.
8. My self-therapist knows as much about psychology as I do.
9. If I want my self-therapist to learn more about psychotherapy, all I have to do is find that information and read it.

24
Self-Therapy Techniques

To improve your self-therapy techniques, it is important to understand a few basic Gestalt therapy techniques developed by Fritz Perls (1969a, 1969b, 1973):
1. Projection. Projection is the most valuable contribution Freud made. Fully understanding projection is very important. I know very little about other people and things. I may know if the person is male or female. I may know what that person has told me. However, that is all I know. Most of what I think I know is only a projection onto that person what I know about myself. I can look at other people and talk about them. I can fantasize about them all I want. Therefore, I can learn about myself by looking at people and talking about myself as that person. I can then look at those statements I make talking about those people and all the things I believe I know about them. I can examine those statements to see if they could also be true about me. If they are true about me, I can own them as mine. If they are not true about me, I can

throw them away or simply let go of them. In this way, I can learn about myself. Learning about myself is what psychotherapy is all about. This learning about myself, or psychotherapy by myself, is what I call self-therapy.

I have taken this a step farther. I do a lot of driving, which in the past was very boring. Now, I find driving alone to be very interesting and I learn a lot when I am alone. As I drive down the freeway, I look for objects, things, people, dogs, birds, billboards, etc. I then use all of these things to learn about myself using projection.

I like billboards most of all because, in the past, I sold advertising and designed advertisements. I can become the ad, all the characters in the ad, and even the person that created the ad. Most billboards are absolutely worthless as far as advertising is concerned. I especially dislike the MTA ads. I don't know what they are thinking. The MTA billboards are simply a waste of money. The best billboards are on Sunset Boulevard in West Hollywood. The reason for this is that the billboard companies have been trained to place liberal ads in liberal neighborhoods and conservative ads in conservative neighborhoods. Even the Los Angeles Times prints liberal news for liberal neighborhoods, the Westside section for example, and conservative news for conservative neighborhoods. Of course, everyone reads what they want to read and everyone sees what they want to see.

In this way, as I drive my car, I notice only those things that I want to notice. I then become what I notice and talk about myself. I own what I want to own and let go of what I don't want to own. What if I make the wrong decision?

It does not matter; I can let go of things as many times as I want until I am ready to own them. However, simply owning everything is the easiest thing to do.
2. Change language. Changing language will change thinking. Changing my thinking by myself is what self-therapy is all about. Changing my language, as Fritz Perls (1969b) suggested is a very good start. However, don't stop there. I can change my language anyway I want. Creating new words can become a valuable pastime. I am surprised at how many words in this book are not in my computer's dictionary.
3. Here and now. Living in the here and now will also change thinking. Most people live in the past or in the future. They obsess about mistakes they made. They plan what they will do when they retire. It is hard to believe that the past and future is all a fantasy. Here and now is all that exists; everything else is only a fantasy. I can live in a fantasy world like everyone else or I can become a real person by living in the here and now.
4. Choice. My life is constantly changed by the many choices I make. Choosing whether to get a BA in science or a BA in theology will change my thinking for the rest of my life. Most people do not realize how many small choices make big changes in their life.
5. Feelings. All feelings are chosen and positive. I choose my feelings by telling myself a statement. If I want to change my feelings, all I have to do is to find that statement and change that statement. In fact, look at all the messages that you are telling yourself and see how you can change the message into a positive message.

6. "Everything I do, I do only for myself," is a quote from Fritz Perls (1969b). Most people believe they are doing things for other people instead of realizing that they are doing things for other people to make themselves feel better.
7. Education. I cannot say enough about education. Education is a lifelong process. Education will change the way a person thinks. My choices in what classes I take will change the way I think. I was a completely different person when I graduated from college compared with the person I was when I started. Graduating from college is a life-changing event. Education can also be a part-time job. When I started school in 1971, I was working full time at $4 an hour. I worked days and went to school at night. Tuition was $50 a semester. As a veteran, the VA paid me $1,200 a semester for going to school. That may not sound like very much to you, but in 1971 I was earning $144 a week minus taxes, working full time. The VA now pays far more than that for school.

    Now, every student earning less than $39,000 a year is entitled to receive a federal grant of up to $5,300 a year. If more money is needed, you may apply for low-interest student loans with no payments due until after graduation. Community colleges in Southern California only cost $13 a semester when requesting a BOG. In other words, you can get paid for going to school and the education you receive will change your life.
8. Jobs. Changing jobs will change the way a person thinks.
9. Location. Changing location will change my life.
10. Relationships. Changing relationships changed my life.
    11. Friends. Changing friends has changed my life.

12. Internet. The Internet has changed my life. I can also use the Internet to change my life. For example, I found my present job on the Internet.
13. Religion. Religion is just like language. We get whatever our parents have when we are born. When we become educated, we may want to let go of some of the beliefs that our parents gave us. Letting go of our parents' beliefs and changing what we believe will change not only our lives, it will also change our children's lives.
14. Diet. Become a vegan or vegetarian. You will see food in a new way. Not only will it change your life, it will also add twenty years on to your life.
15. Exercise. Exercise will change and lengthen your life.
16. Jogging. Jogging actually changes the chemicals in the brain.
17. Explore. You are not going to meet people while sitting in your living room watching television. Go places as often as possible. Meet new people and they will change your life.
18. Read. Read everything you can that is nonfiction, especially science. Education is a lifelong process. Use your brain or lose it.
19. Write. Reading is only an excuse for not writing. As soon as you have read enough, start writing. You know far more than you think you do.

25
Genetics

The human genome is made up of about 19,000 genes (de Investigaciones Oncol, C. 2014). Ninety-nine percent of all human genes existed fifty million years before the existence of primates, which started about eighty-five million years ago (de Investigaciones Oncol, C. 2014). Therefore, the genes that are causing us trouble today, both medical and behavioral, have been with us for more than one hundred thirty-five millions of years, long before we became human and even before we became primates.

What were our ancestors like one hundred thirty-five million years ago? They were mammals, about six inches long, and looked very much like a mouse. They lived in tunnels in the ground and ate mostly insects. Although they lived with the dinosars, they were probably unnoticed by them. They probably were nocturnal and ran into their tunnels at any jarring of the ground or sound. I know that it is hard to believe, but they also had the same phobias and psychological problems that we have today. Their looks and size was about the only thing that separated them from us. We are 99 percent the same. We had even more genes in common with them than we do with the present day chimpanzees, with which we have 98.7 percent of our genes in common (Morris et al. 2010; Olson, M. V., and Varki, A. 2003). It is believed that chimpanzees are evolving faster than humans and away from humans, because they reproduce faster.

There are two hypotheses about human genetics (Gillham 2011). The Common Disease/ Common Variant hypothesis is that only one or a few alleles predispose a specific disease. These variants or mutations may or may not be selectively advantageous (Reich 2001). The Genetic Heterogeneity or Multiple Rare Variant Model Hypotheses is that susceptibility results from multiple rare variants or mutations in many genes (Bodmer 2008). I believe that both of these hypotheses are correct. The frequency of the gene variation depends on the potential to produce offspring and its selective advantage for survival.

All this can also be applied to human behavior. For example, a gene mutation giving an ancestor a phobia of snakes gives that ancestor a survival advantage and that snake phobia gene is passed to descendants. The same is true for germ phobia, spider phobia, fear of heights, etc. Therefore, the Common Disease/Common Variant Hypothesis could be applied to most specific phobias. Whereas the Genetic Heterogeneity or Multiple Rare Variant Model Hypothesis could be applied to schizophrenia, bipolar disorder, somatoform disorder, autistic spectrum disorder, tourette's, homosexuality, etc.

Every aspect of behavior, health and disease is controlled or influenced by our genes (Gillham 2011). However, my genetic destiny is not preordained. I no longer have to be a victim of my genes. For as little as $99 (23andMe.com), I can now have genetic testing to find out what my genetic blueprint looks like. For example, one in six men have the gene for prostate cancer (Gillham 2011). If I happen to have the gene for prostate cancer, I do not have to die of prostate cancer. Finding out with genetic testing that I have the gene for prostate cancer will motivate me to have my prostate tested regularly and have it removed at the first sign of trouble. However, eventually something will be discovered early so that my prostate can be removed to save my life. In this way, genetic testing may allow me to live many years longer.

Most of my life I have struggled with a germ phobia. I believed all that nonsense about phobias being learned by conditioning and reinforcement. I tried systematic desensitization with little effect. I tried to remember things from my childhood that may have given me a germ phobia. Could my mother have given me a germ phobia by teaching me to wash my hands and not eat apples from a tree without washing the apples first? Then I learned that having a germ phobia is genetic. If a person does not have the gene, they will not have the phobia. Finally, I was able to understand my behavior. Now, whenever my germ phobia kicks in, I know it is my genes. I can then laugh at my genes and ignore them. I no longer have a problem due to my understanding of what is going on with me.

New discoveries in human genetics are changing everything (Gillham 2011). Soon, parents will be told everything about their child as soon as the pregnancy is discovered. A sample will be taken for genetic testing and the parents will then go to a website and read all about their child. The website will tell the parents about all the genetic mutations that their child has. This will give the parents a choice of having the child or aborting the child and trying for a genetically better child.

The parents will be told how long the child will live and the probable cause of death, whether the child will die of heart disease or cancer, even what kind of cancer. They will be told the child's sexual orientation, specific phobias the child will have, whether the child be schizophrenic, bipolar, or depressed. Most importantly, they will be told what illnesses the child will suffer from throughout their life (Gillham 2011).

It is now known that almost everything is genetic and can be read by genetic testing. Don't ask what is genetic, ask what is not genetic. For example, AIDS is a virus and not genetic. However, scientists have discovered that about 10 percent of Americans with European ancestry have a genetic immunity to the HIV virus (Gillham 2011). How can this be when most people believe that HIV came from Africa? There is a theory about that, which I also happen to believe (Gillham 2011, Brown 2011, Yong 2011, Abi-Rached 2011).

About 500 thousand years ago a group of Africans went to Europe where they lived in isolation from Africans for about 470 thousand years. During that time, some of their genes mutated, improving their immune system and making them larger, stronger, and appear white with black hair or fur. The vitamin D hypothesis is wrong. Six or more genes determine skin color (Gillham 2011). That group of Europeans are now called Neanderthals. During that time, gene mutations of Africans also improved their immune system. Then, about 30 thousand years ago, another group of Africans migrated to Europe where they "intermarried" with the Neanderthals. Then, about 10 thousand years ago, a great plague swept across Europe, possibly the black plague. All of the Neanderthals and all of the Africans died because their immune systems were not sufficient enough to prevent their death. Those in Europe that survived the plague did so only because they had acquired the immune systems from both the Neanderthals and the Africans. This meant that they were descendants from both Neanderthals and Africans and had inherited the genes for their immune system from both groups. This means that most Europeans and Americans with European ancestors evolved from both Neanderthals and Africans and have the immune systems of both groups. In addition to this, during the last 10 thousand years, in Europe there were many plagues and epidemics including the black plague and smallpox that killed all those without the best immune systems. Even in the United States, we have had many epidemics such as smallpox. All these epidemics have left the survivors descendants with improved immune systems. Possibly a gene mutation that aided in the survival of smallpox also gives a person immunity to HIV.

I have always believed that many things were genetic. However, it surprised me to find out that most behavior is also genetic. For example, a simple little thing like how a person crosses their arms is genetic. Previously, it was believed that children learned how to cross their arms by watching their parents. Now, we know that children cross their arms like their parents because they both have the same genetic mutation.

John Watson believed that all babies are born exactly the same and referred to them as a "blank slate" on which anything could be written by parents and teachers. This belief dominated American thinking for many years. Now, we know that this is total nonsense. Every person is genetically different, including identical twins. Our behavior, looks, and health are all genetic. Almost every health problem a person has before age fifty is genetic, and many problems after age fifty are genetic. Sixty percent of all children going to the hospital are only going there because of their genetic mutations (Gillham 2011). In addition, 20 percent of children only go to the hospital for genetic immunity mutations. Only 9 percent of all human embryos have a normal set of chromosomes. Seventy percent of all human embryos have major structural chromosomal abnormalities. About 1 in 200 human conceptions have an additional number 21 chromosome, which results in more than 400 genes occurring in triplicate. That leads to intellectual disabilities and physical defects known as Down syndrome. Almost every behavior a person has is genetic.

The question is not what is genetic, the question is what is not genetic. For example, Polio is not genetic. Germs and viruses are real health problems that can also change behavior. However, cancer, heart disease, blood pressure, diabetes, and most health problems are all genetic. Thinking of a behavior that is not genetic is extremely hard. For example, children get whichever religion their parents have when they are born. However, a gene has been discovered that determines how religious a person is—sort of a religious fanaticism gene.

People seem very resistant to the idea that most behavior

is genetic. They believe that eye color and hair color is genetic, but if you say cancer, heart disease, diabetes, schizophrenia, and homosexuality is genetic, they say, "No way." People seem to think genetics is only an opinion and that everyone has an opinion, similar to political opinion. I am always amazed at how much people discount scientific facts.

People *want* to believe that they have created their children to be the way they want them to be. People *want* to believe that children are the product of parental training, education, and religion when in fact children are the products of their genes, which they get from their biological parents and not from their adoptive parents.

Starting in 2010, all babies born in the United States are being tested for 29 genetic diseases when they could be tested for 7,000 genetic diseases at almost no additional cost. Why is that? Some people in the government believe that it would be cruel to tell parents that their children have a genetic disease for which there is no cure. Therefore, babies may only be genetically tested for the 29 genetic diseases for which we now have a cure. If we do not have a cure, it cannot be tested for. Also, all genetic material must be destroyed immediately when it could be stored forever until needed. Some people are paranoid about storing five drops of blood from their children.

How do we cure genetic diseases? The best cure is prevention. Any couple wanting a child should have genetic testing before conception to determine what diseases they possess, and more specifically, what recessive genes they have in common. If they do possess a recessive genetic disease, they should use IVF and remove as many eggs as possible and fertilize them with sperm. After conception, test every embryo to find one that does not have the genetic disease of the parents and then place that embryo back into the mother. However, if the parents' genetic testing found no genetic disease, the embryo should also be tested as soon after conception as possible. If the embryo test finds a genetic disease, then the parents may choose to abort and try for a genetically better child and improve their lives. If they choose not to abort, they will know what disease their child will have, what to expect, and find help for that child before the child is born.

In addition to our genes controlling our behavior and medical problems, we are also making important choices based solely on our genes. Researchers at the University of California, San Diego, and Yale University studied the genomes of 2,000 individuals and their friends and found that people have more genes in common with their friends (Paddock, C. 2014, July 15). The genes of friends that are most common control the sense of smell (Paddock, C. 2014, July 15). This means that friends are smelling food the same and may enjoy the same kinds of food and possibly prefer the same restaurants. If we take this idea back 135 million years ago at a time when our ancestors had the same genes that we have now, friends may have been searching for food and eating together. In addition, new research with over 26,000 people aged fifty and over, found that married couples have more genes in common (Whiteman, H. 2014, May 25). This adds another reason for couples to check their genomes before having children. Recessive genes in common with mates are our children's biggest problem.

On March 2, 2012, I took the plunge and paid $99 plus

tax to 23andme.com to have my genes tested. They mailed me a tube to spit in and I mailed it back the same day I received it. On April 1, 2012, I received the results online at their website 23andme.com. I found both good news and bad news. I have about 9 percent higher than average chance of having prostate cancer, which means I should have my prostate checked regularly. I have a gene for overeating and a gene to be obese. I have never been obese. However, I do weigh 180 lbs., which is more than I have ever weighed before. It is now time to go on a diet. I have a 9 percent higher than average risk of developing type 2 diabetes, if I allow myself to become obese.

On the upside, I have the longevity gene, which means I will live to be ninety-five or older, if I do not become obese or ignore my prostate. I also have genes for not having Alzheimer's and Parkinson's disease. That is a great relief because my grandmother had Parkinson's and I was sure that I had inherited it. Not having Alzheimer's is a great relief for someone expected to live to ninety-five or older.

However, the great majority of my genes turned out to be average and normal, which is both expected and boring. My ancestry is 100 percent Northern European, meaning that all of my ancestors came from Germany, Netherlands, France, Ireland, Scotland, and England. I have 2.7 percent Neanderthal genes, where 2.5 percent is the average for persons of Northern European ancestry.

23andMe also has a service in which they compare the genes of all the people they have tested so far and identify close genetic matches as possibly being relatives. This relative finder lists all close matches and tells you if they are third, fourth, or fifth cousins. They identified about 1,000 people as genetically being cousins of mine. I am now corresponding with several of these new cousins.

What is environmental and not genetic?
1. Germs and viruses are real problems. Viruses can even cause genetic mutations.
2. Radiation
3. Solar radiation
4. Toxins
5. Temperature. Hot water, such as hot tubs, should be avoided by those who might get pregnant or are pregnant.
6. Which religion you have.
7. Oxygen
8. Food
9. X-rays and CAT scans
10. Radon gas
11. Toxic chemicals such as aflatoxins.
12. A staggering list of prescription drugs.
13. Fetal Alcohol Syndrome.

Mutagens of Genes:

Benzo(a)pyrene is the major mutagen of genes today (Gillham 2011). It is one of fifteen mutagen chemicals found in tobacco smoke, making smoking tobacco the biggest mutagen known today (McCann 1976; Florin 1980). Benzo(a)pyrene is also found in soot, diesel exhaust fumes, automobile exhaust fumes, coal tar, burnt toast, and cooked meats (Gillham 2011).

Permanent hair dyes contain a variety of mutagens (Ames 1975; Takkouche 2005; Hermann 2007; Gillham 2011).

Ultraviolet light is a mutagen that is not a chemical. Sunlamps emit twelve times the UVA of sunlight. People that use them are 2.5 times more likely to develop squamous cell carcinoma (Gillham 2011).

Radiation is a mutagen that can mutate your genes or kill you. For example, all US tank shells are now coated with depleted uranium, which is made from the waste of nuclear power plants. Hitting steel with a tank shell covered with nuclear waste makes that shell burn right into the steal. US soldiers riding in tanks are being radiated with the nuclear waste changing their genes and radiating their wives with radioactive semen, mutating their wives. Who knows what their children will be like? Many US soldiers have been exposed to nuclear waste. The only reason nuclear power plants were created was to generate nuclear waste for the military. It takes more energy to build a nuclear power plant than the energy that comes out. Who knows what the cost would be if a power plant had a meltdown in the United States.

De novo genes are basically genes that people have that neither of their parents possess. How can this be, when we inherit our genes from our parents? Most people believe that the system of creating a child is perfect and half its genes come from each parent. Instead, the process of creating a child is extremely poor. It is so bad that eighty percent of all embryos are aborted before the mother knows she is pregnant, because they are deformed fetuses that cannot survive. There is a minimum of one hundred and fifty de novo genes in every one of us and many people have far more de novo genes than that. De novo genes can be divided into three basic groups: mutations, duplications and deletions.

Mutations are mistakes made in genes, which can be one base pair or many base pairs. Some mutations cause death. Some mutations cause harm and are noticed. However, most of these mutations cause no harm and are never noticed. These mistakes are then passes on to children.

Duplications (or repeats) are mistakes in which whole genes (or partial genes) are duplicated. The gene may be duplicate once or many times. One duplication causes no problem and is not even noticed. However, when the duplication continues many times it then causes a problem that is noticed. Also, the higher the number of duplications, the younger the problem will show up in a person. The lower the number of duplications, the older the problem will show up in a person. Also, the number of repeats usually increases when passed on to a child, giving the problem to the child at a younger age than the parent.

Duplications are the driving force behind evolution. When a gene is mutated or deleted it can cause death of the fetus. Whereas, when the gene duplicates, there is no problem with the fetus. After many generations, the duplicated gene may mutate to create a new gene while the original gene controls the original trait outcome with no problem is noticed. As time passes with many generations, the original gene may be deleted and the duplicate gene takes over with improved traits. Over millions of years and many generations the descendants slowly change. Therefore de novo duplications are extremely important.

Deletions are missing genes caused by mistakes and responsible for the biggest problems. The missing genes can be anything and therefore are the biggest cause of death in the fetus. Some deletions cause great harm and the fetus lives. The missing genes may be responsible for anything and will be passed on to children. The biggest problem is that when the father's genes are matched up with the mother's genes to form base pairs, whenever a deletion is encountered, the other parent's genes are kicked out, until the end of the deletion and then pairing resumes. This means that the gene is missing from both parents and there is no gene trait for that deletion. Therefore, there is something completely missing from the person and they have no idea what is missing. De novo gene deletions are believed to be responsible for all of the big five problems in psychology: schizophrenia, bi-polar, depression, ASD and ADHD. Many other psychological disorders are also caused by deletions.

What is the cure? The cure is to find what gene is deleted or mutated and replace it in the person's genome in every cell in their body with the correct gene. This has been done with mice and experiments are now being done with humans. However, we were born to soon. In the future this procedure will be common.

26
A Few Ways to Improve Your Life

1. Let go of all those things your parents, teachers and other adults told you and fulfill your own genetic blueprint.
2. Education is a lifelong process. Continually sign up for classes. Nothing increases neurogenesis and intelligence more than continual education.
3. Eat all the RAW fruits and vegetables you can get your hands on.
4. Decrease calorie intake by drinking water and unsweetened drinks, such as tea without sugar.
5. Get your own personal genome at 23andme.com.
6. Read at least two nonfiction books a month about what you are most interested in. However, reading is only an excuse for not writing.
7. Write a book summarizing what you have been reading.
8. Eliminate all caffeine by drinking only drinks that are

caffeine free. Never drink coffee unless it is caffeine free. Never eat coffee ice cream.
9. Eliminate all alcohol.
10. Eliminate all tobacco products.
11. Take up jogging or at least walking.
12. Take up bicycle riding.
13. Take up roller skating or skateboarding.
14. Take up horseshoe pitching. In addition to being great exercise, horseshoe pitching is another form of meditation. It will take your mind off of everything. I am a lifetime member of the National Horseshoe Pitchers Association. Even the people you meet will improve your life. You can find local horseshoe pitching simply by going to horseshoepitching.com and clicking on your local area. There are many horseshoe-pitching clubs everywhere.
15. Learn all about Tax Lien Certificates. Tax Lien Certificates can increase your income at very little risk depending on which state you live in.
16. Use projection for self-therapy as explained in a previous chapter.
17. Take long hikes in the mountains or without the mountains.
18. Get a pet to talk to. Everyone needs someone to talk to. Most pets communicate very well. My cat understands everything I tell him.
19. Sleep longer and enjoy your dreams.
20. Flossing your teeth every day can add up to 6.4 years to your life, according to Michael Roizen, MD, author of RealAge.
21. Take the stairs instead of the elevator.

22. Read a book while walking or walk while reading a book for a minimum of thirty minutes every day.
23. Learn to choose your feelings by changing the message you are telling yourself. All feelings are chosen.
24. Let go of the past. It does not exist. Live your life in the here and now.
25. Spend more time with nature by hiking, fishing, and camping, or simply set in the park and watch the birds and squirrels.
26. Stop eating ice cream and milk shakes. We don't even know the contents.
27. Pretend that donuts are poison.
28. Learn more information about human growth hormones and vitamins.
29. Try something different.
30. Don't stop yourself.
31. Learn to create multiple streams of income. Find many ways to make a little income from the Internet. Information is very valuable. Sell some information on the Internet. Most people will pay $1 for anything. Many people paying $1 adds up very quickly. Simply learning how to do this will improve your thinking.
32. Grow some of your own food.
33. Do not drink liquids containing sugar or corn syrup. Do not drink diet sodas.
34. Vote in every election and vote only for politicians that want to help poor people and vote against politicians that want to help the wealthy and corporations.
35. Have another child or adopt one.
36. Start a new business. Businesses make great tax deductions.

37. Start a nonprofit organization.
38. Buy a metal detector and start a ring collection. The beach is full of lost jewelry. Be sure to buy one that can be used underwater. Only buy one with a digital display. I bought a Garrett AT-Gold and found sixteen rings in my first fourteen weeks. Although, I understand that the Garrett AT-Pro is better for use in salt water.
39. Find things to do and reasons to get out of the house. A home is a place to sleep, not a place to live your life.
40. Find ways to liberate your brain.
41. Study those things that interest you the most.
42. Buy a kayak and go fishing.
43. Don't bring a knife to a gunfight.

27
The Definition of Behavior

Most people disagree with me when I say that "behavior is genetic." Most people seem to resist this idea. They believe that genetics is very important, but do not believe that behavior is genetic. When discussing this with them more, I found that their definition of the word behavior is very different from what I think behavior is. Evidently psychologists think of behavior in a different way than the average person.

For example, another instructor said that he is a volunteer working with gang members, changing their behavior. With his counseling, they completely change their behavior and drop out of the gang. According to him, gang behavior is not genetic and is simply learned from other kids in the neighborhood. He believes that all behavior is learned and can be changed by learning better behavior.

I had not even considered gang behavior to be a behavior. This simply does not meet my definition of what behavior is. Like most psychologists, I look at unusual behavior, figure out how that person got that behavior, and then apply that same reasoning to normal behavior. My definition of behavior is something specific that a person does, such as crossing arms, writing with their right hand, etc. I do not consider gang behavior to be a behavior. In my way of thinking, if the gang member had a gene to become a leader, then he will eventually become the gang's leader. If he is not in a gang and is in the Lions Club, he will eventually become president of the Lions Club. I do not consider gang behavior to be a behavior. So, what is the definition that I use for behavior? Well, I use the same definition that other psychologists use. Well, what is that definition? I did not know. So, I looked it up on the Internet. As it turns out, many psychologists have been struggling with the definition of behavior. A group of 125 psychologists were asked to come up with a definition of behavior. At first they could not agree on a definition. Finally they changed the definition until a majority agreed with that definition. That definition is the following: "Behavior is the internally coordinated responses (actions or inactions) of whole living organisms (individuals or groups) to internal and/or external stimuli, excluding developmental change."

When I think about behavior, I think about two specific groups of behavior, The Big Five personality traits for normal behavior and all the behavior disorders listed in the DSM-IV for abnormal behavior. The Big Five personality traits each also have six individual components, making a total of thirty normal personality traits. They are:

- Extraversion
- Warmth
- Gregariousness

- Assertiveness
- Activity
- Excitement-seeking
- Positive emotions
- Agreeableness/aggression
- Trust
- Straightforwardness
- Altruism
- Compliance
- Modesty
- Tender mindedness
- Conscientiousness/dependability
- Competence
- Order
- Dutifulness
- Achievement-striving
- Self-discipline
- Deliberation
- Emotional Stability/Neuroticism
- Anxiety
- Hostility
- Depression
- Self-consciousness
- Impulsiveness
- Vulnerability
- Openness to experience/culture/intellect
- Fantasy
- Aesthetics
- Feelings
- Actions

- Ideas
- Values

In addition to these, the following behaviors have been studied:
- Positive emotionality
- Negative emotionality
- Constraint
- Intelligence

Psychological interests:
- Realistic
- Investigative
- Artistic
- Social
- Enterprising
- Conventional

Social attitudes:
- Conservatism
- Right-wing authoritarianism
- Religiousness

Psychiatric behavior disorders listed in the DSM-IV:
- Depression
- Major depressive disorder
- Dysthymia.
- Panic disorder
- Anxiety disorders
- Generalized anxiety disorder

- Obsessive-compulsive disorder
- Post-traumatic Stress disorder
- Specific phobias
- Social phobias
- Agoraphobia
- Alcoholism
- Antisocial behavior
- Bipolar disorder
- Panic disorder
- Psychosomatic disorder
- Somataform disorders
- Somatization disorder
- Conversion disorder
- Hypochondriasis
- Body dysmorphic disorder
- Dissociative disorders
- Dissociative amnesia
- Dissociative fugue
- Dissociative identity disorder (multiple personality disorder)
- Depersonalization disorder
- Sexual dysfunction
- Sexual desire disorders
- Orgasmic disorders
- Premature ejaculation
- Vaginismus
- Paraphilias
- Fetishism
- Voyeurism
- Exhibitionism

- Frontteurism
- Transvestite fetishism
- Sexual sadism
- Sexual masochism
- Pedophilia
- Gender-identity disorders
- Schizoid personality disorder
- Paranoid personality disorder
- Dependent personality disorder
- Avoidant personality disorder
- Narcissistic personality disorder
- Borderline personality disorder
- Antisocial personality disorder
- Schizophrenic disorders
- Disorganized schizophrenia
- Catatonic schizophrenia
- Paranoid schizophrenia
- Undifferentiated schizophrenia
- Attention-deficit hyperactivity disorder
- Autistic disorder
- Autistic spectrum disorder

In addition to all these behaviors, I am willing to add a few more:
- Sexual Orientation
- Sleep
- Memory
- Arousal
- Motivation
- Pleasure

- Pain
- Eating
- Drug addiction
- Emotion
- Excitability
- Sexual behavior
- Ability to concentrate
- Reaction to stress
- Desire for companionship
- Emotional reactivity
- Ability to learn
- Ability to resist disease
- Mate selection
- Motion sickness
- Sleep talking
- Sleepwalking
- Insomnia
- Sleep apnea
- Narcolepsy
- Susceptibility to hypnosis
- Obesity
- Diet
- Tourette's Syndrome
- Arm crossing
- Tongue rolling

This is a list of about 135 specific behaviors that have been studied more than any other behaviors. All of them have been found to be significantly affected by genetics, while the environmental affect was found to be insignificant or minimal at most (Bouchard 2004). The biggest environmental affect is malnutrition. Malnutrition can lower IQ scores of very young children. However, by adolescence, the child has caught up and there is no longer any environmental affect on IQ scores. Environmental stimulation is the same, although lack of environmental stimulation can lower the IQ scores of very young children, it is only temporary and IQ is unaffected by adolescents.

What is meant by "significantly affected by genetics" (Bouchard 2004)? This is understood to mean genetic by two standard deviations, in other words 95 percent genetic and not 100 percent genetic, because there are always a few exceptions to everything. However, environmental effects were also found to be only 5 percent or less. The environment can freeze the child to death, but it cannot make him right or left handed, gay or straight.

I simply do not understand the people believing that behavior is determined by the environment. How could simply living in West Hollywood make a person gay? I would think it would be more likely for a gay person to make a choice of moving to West Hollywood simply because they are gay.

I CAN CHANGE MY BEHAVIOR IF I WANT TO CHANGE MY BEHAVIOR

Even though I have a germ phobia, I can change that behavior if I want to change that behavior. Once I discovered that my germ phobia was genetic, I knew I could ignore my genetics and do whatever I wanted to do. Genetic behavior is what I do when I am not thinking about my behavior. When

I focus my full attention on my behavior, I can do anything I want to do. However, why bother? It is easier to simply observe my behavior and accept that my behavior is OK just as it is. OR, I can choose to ignore my genetics and do anything I want to do. My genetics and the environment do not control my behavior. I control my behavior. I can do anything I want to do.

28
A Little About the Past and the Future

While serving in the U.S. Army in Korea (1965-1967) as an Ordinance Supply Specialist (46D20), part of my job was to write, on IBM cards, orders for vehicle parts needed for repair. Those cards were then placed in a card-punch machine and holes were punched in the cards according to what I wrote on the cards. Those cards were then put in a card reader and the information was transmitted back to the states by telephone line. That experience led to my interest in computers and my deciding to become a computer programmer after getting out of the army.

In 1968, I enrolled at the Computer Programming Institute in Indianapolis to learn computer programming. I learned Basic Assembly Language (BAL), Common Business Oriented Language (COBAL), and how to operate the best computer at the time, the IBM 360. It was a large mainframe computer with 360k mostly used by big banks. After graduation, I found that only a couple of IBM 360s were in Indiana and no jobs were available. I left Indiana and moved to Los Angeles, where most of the IBM 360s were located. I found very few of them and no job. I finally took a job working for Blue Chip Stamps and quickly moved up to supervisor.

In 1970 I met Nicolas Leoni, a very good friend who straightened out my thinking about politics. At that time, he was a student at California State University, Northridge. He eventually got a PhD and worked there as a professor for about forty years. Anyway, he also told me that the best place to pick up chicks was college, so I enrolled at Los Angeles Pierce College only to pick up chicks. He was right and I continued taking classes. After I had sixty-eight units, including fifteen units of computer programming, I transferred to California State University, Northridge, where I received a bachelor of arts degree in psychology (1975). I then got a master of arts degree in counseling psychology from Goddard College in Plainfield, Vermont (1980). All through school I did all my work including my master's thesis on a typewriter. I did not buy my first computer until the Macintosh 512 came out, which cost me about $1,000 and came with no software. It had only 512k memory, so I paid $2,000 to have it upgraded to a Monster Mac with 4meg of memory. I then spent $2,000 on software and paid $2,400 for my first printer. I also spent $1,200 for my first FAX machine. There was no Internet at that time.

You and I have had the misfortune to have been born too soon. Everything will be much better in the future. People will be living like many movies such as *Artificial Intelligence* and *The Minority Report* are portraying the future. Advertisements will say our names as we pass by. Computers will be implanted under our skin and we will wear them continually. I will be able to read the screen on the lower half of my glasses.

The biggest change in the future will be healthcare, and genetics will be the driving force. Very soon, much sooner they you believe, genetics will force the government to take over all healthcare in the United States and make health insurance obsolete. Health insurance companies are the most disgusting corporations in the world. I don't know why people have put up with their nonsense so long. The federal government taking over all healthcare in the United States will be the greatest achievement in our lifetime. Trips to doctors and hospitals will be cut in half or possibly decreased as much as 80 percent. Major health problems will disappear and doctors will have very little to do. There will still be car accidents and cuts to take care of, but major health problems will be a thing of the past. How is this going to happen? Genetics!

When people are educated about genetics, every prospective parent will have their complete genome paid for by the federal government. I had my genome done in February 2012 for $99 plus tax. Once the federal government starts doing them for every person for free, the cost the government pays will come way down. The prospective parents will then receive free genetic counseling. This will be a great savings to the federal government.

Right now, every child born in the United States is required to have genetic testing after it is born. However, at the present time, genetic testing is only allowed to test for the twenty-nine problems for which we have a cure. Any health problem the child may have in which there is no cure is not allowed to be tested for. There are about 7,000 devastating genetic diseases that can be tested for at the same cost. Why don't they test for all 7,000 genetic diseases at the same time? Because, the Republicans believe that it would be cruel to tell parents that their child has a devastating genetic disease for which there is no cure. Therefore, the testing for those 7,000 devastating genetic diseases is not allowed even though the cost would be same.

However, very soon genetics will force the federal government to set up a huge genetic database with the genomes of every person in the United States plus many others from outside the United States. Soon every person will be able to walk into any health clinic without an appointment and ask to see a doctor free of charge. The doctor will punch into a computer on his desk the social security number of that person into the federal database and read everything about that person before he sees them. The computer will tell the doctor the person's complete health history and complete genome. It will tell the doctor what has happened in the past and what will happen to that person in the future before the doctor has seen that person. When the doctor meets the patient he will explain to the patient what the computer told him and check for those problems.

Psychiatric problems as well as health problems will no longer be referred to by their symptoms. Both psychiatric problems and health problems will be referred to by their gene number. The doctor will not talk to you about breast cancer. The doctor will talk about BRCA1 or BRCA2.

Thank You

I want to thank you for reading this book. I know how valuable your time is. I only hope that you learned something that will improve your life. I have devoted my life to genetic research and psychology. I am working on a new book, which I intend to publish as soon as possible. Watch for it and email me at schpa1st@gmail.com and I will try to answer all your questions. Please follow me on twitter @jimatwellauthor.

I also want to thank all the students at Platt College, Los Angeles, for helping me write this book. I learned a great deal from you. The cover of this book was designed by Elvis Chung, a student at Platt College, Los Angeles. Thank you, Elvis Chung. Most of this book was written between classes at Platt College, Los Angeles.

Thank You,
James L. Atwell

Bibliography

Af Bjerken, S., F. Marschinke, and I. Stromberg. "Inhibition of Astrocytes Promotes Long-Distance Growing Nerve Fibers in Ventral Mesencephalic Cultures." *International Journal of Developmental Neuroscience* 26 (2008): 683-691.

Abi-Rached, Jobin, Kulkami, McWhinnie, Dalva, Gragert, Babrzadeh, Gharizadeh, Luo, Plummer, Kimani, Carrington, Middleton, Rajalingam, Beksac, Marsh, Maiers, Guethlein, Tavoularis, Little, Green, Norman, and Parham. "The Shaping of Modern Human Immune Systems by Multiregional Admixture with Archaic Humans." *Science* Magazine (2011). http://dx.doi.org/10.1126/science.1209202

Amedi, A., L. B. Merabet, F. Bermpohl, and A. Pascual-Leone. "The Occipital Cortex in the Brain: Lessons About Plasticity and Vision." *Current Directions in Psychological Science* 14 (2005): 306-311.

Ames, Bruce N., H. O. Kammen, and Edith Yamasaki. "Hair Dyes Are Mutagenic: Identification of a Variety of Mutagenic Ingredients." *Proceedings of the National Academy of Sciences of the United States* 72 (1975): 2423-2427.

Antrobus, John S., Judith S. Antrobus, and J. L. Singer. "Eye Movements Accompanying Daydreaming, Visual Imagery, and Thought Suppression." *Journal of Abnormal and Social Psychology* 69 (1964): 244-252.

Antrobus, Judith S., W. Dement, and C. Fisher. "Patterns of Dreaming and Dream Recall." *Journal of Abnormal and Social Psychology* 69 (1964): 341-344.

Antrobus, Judith S., John S. Antrobus, and Charles Fisher. "Psychoanalytic Implications of Recent Research on Sleep and Dreaming - Part 1: Empirical Findings." *Journal of the American Psychoanalytic Association* 13 (1965): 197-270.

Arkin, Arthur M., John S. Antrobus, Max F. Toth, Julia Baker, and Frances Jackler. "A Comparison of the Content of Mentation Reports Elicited After Non Rapid Eye Movements (NREM) Associated Sleep Utterance and NREM 'Silent' Sleep,'" *Journal of Nervous & Mental Disease* 155, no. 6 (1972): 427-435.

Atwell, James. "Dreams, Dreaming & Sleep." Masters Thesis, Goddard College, (1980).

Beck, Henry W. "Dream Analysis in Family Therapy." *Clinical Social Work Journal* 5, no. 1 (1977): 53-57.

Benjamin, Geoffrey. *Temiar Religion*. University of Singapore, 1969.

Bodmer, Walter and Carolina Bonilla. "Common and Rare Variants in Multifactorial Susceptibility to Common Diseases." *Nature Genetics,* 40 (2008): 695-701.

Boring, E. G. *A History of Experimental Psychology*. Second edition. New York: Appleton, 1950.

Bouchard, Thomas J., Jr. "Genetic Influence on Human Psychological Traits A Survey." *Current Directions in Psychological Research* 13, no. 4 (2004): 148-151.

Branden, Nathaniel Ph.D. *The Power of Self-Esteem*, Deerfield Beach, Florida, 1992. Health Communications, Inc.

Brenner, C. *An Elementary Textbook of Psychoanalysis*. New York: Anchor, 1974.

Brown, Eryn. "Humans got immunity boost from Neanderthals, study finds." *Los Angeles Times*, August 25, 2011.

Brown, Judith M. & Rosalind D. Cartwright. "Locating NREM Dreaming Through Instrumental Responses." *Psychophysiology* 15, no. 1 (1978): 35-39.

Calogeras, Roy C. "Husband and Wife Exchange of dreams." *International Review of Psychoanalysis* 4, no. 1 (1977): 27, 71-82 .

Cambras, Trinitat, Laudino Lopez, Jorge Luis Arias, and Diez-Noguera. "Quantitative Changes in Neuronal and Glial Cells in the Supraachiasmatic Nucleus as a function of the Lighting Conditions During Weaning." *Developmental Brain Research* 157, no. 1 (June 2005): 27-33.

Camern HA, McKay RD. "Restring Productin of Hippocampal Neurns in ld Age." *Nature Neuroscience* 2 (1999): 894-897.

Cartwright, Rosaland D. *Night Life, Explorations in Dreaming*. Englewood Cliffs: Prentice-Hall, Inc., 1977.

Cayce, Hugh Lynn. *Dreams, The Language of the Unconscious*. Virginia Beach: Edgar Cayce Foundation 1962.

Chait, L. D. "Factors Influencing the Subjective Response to Caffeine." *Behav Pharmacol* 3 (1992): 219-228.

Chandra, Satish. "Repression, Dreaming and Primary Process Thinking: Skinnerian Formulations of Some Freudian Facts." *Behaviorism* 4, no.1 (1976): 53-75.

Clementz, G. L. & J. W. Dailey. "Psychotropic Effects of Caffeine." *Am Fam Physician* 37 (1988): 167-172.

Cohen, David B. "Dream Recall and Total Sleep Time." *Perceptual & Motor Skills* 34, no. 2 (1972): 456-458.

Cohen, David B. "A comparison of Genetic and Social Contributions to Dream Recall Frequency and Social Contributions to Dream Recall Frequency." *Journal of Abnormal Psychology* 82, no. 2a (1973): 368-371.

Cohen, David B. "Sex Role Orientation and Dream Recall." *Journal of Abnormal Psychology* 82, no. 2b (1973): 246-252, 1267-1277.

Cohen, David B. "To Sleep Perchance to Recall a Dream: Repression is Not the Demon Who Conceals and Hoards Our Forgotten Dreams." *Psychology Today* 7, no. 12 (1974): 50-54.

Cohen, David B. "Changes in REM Dream Content During the Night: Implications for a Hypothesis About Changes in Cerebral Dominance Across REM Periods." *Perceptual & Motor Skills* 44, no. 3 (1977): 2, 1267-1277.

Cohen, David B., and Gary Wolfe. "Dream Recall and Repression: Evidence for an Alternative Hypothesis." *Journal of Counseling & Clinical Psychology* 41, no. 3 (1973): 349-355.

Collins, Francis S. *The Language of Life*. New York: HarperCollins Publishers, 2010.

Coxhead, David. *Dreams, Visions of the Night*. London: Thames and Hudson, 1976.

De Becker, Raymond. *The Understanding of Dreams and Their Influence on the History of Man*. New York: Hawthorn Books, Inc., 1968.

De Saint-Denys, Hervey, Schatzman, Morton. *Dreams and How to Guide Them*. Duckworth, 1982.

De Investigaciones Oncol, C. "Over 99% of human protein coding genes have an origin that predates primates by over 50 million years." *Medical News Today*, July 7, 2014. Retrieved from Http://www.mecicalnewstoday.com/releases/279196.php.

Dement, William C. *Some Must Watch While Some Must Sleep*. San Francisco: San Francisco Book Co., Inc., 1976.

Dement, William C., and N. Kleitman. "The Relation of Eye Movements During Sleep to Dream Activity: An Objective Method for the Study of Dreaming." *Journal of Experimental Psychology* 53 (1957): 50, 339-346. Diamond, Edwin. *The Science of Dreams*. New York: Macfadden-Bartel, Inc, 1963.

Domino, George. "Compensatory Aspects of Dreams: An Empirical Test of Jung's Theory." *Journal of Personality & Social Psychology* 34, no. 4 (1976): 658-662.

Downing, Jack. *Dreams and Nightmares*. New York: Harper and Row, 1973.

Doyon, J., and H. Benali. "Reorganization and Plasticity in the Adult Brain During Learning of Motor Skills." *Current Opinion in Neurobiology* 15 (2005): 161-167.

Dufour, Roger. "The Relationship of Investment in the Dream." *Etudes Psychotherapiques* 19 (1975): 19-27.

Duman R. S., S. Nakagawa, and J. Malberg. "Regulation of Adult Neurgenesis by Antidepressant Treatment." *Neuropsychopharmacology* 25 (2001): 836-844.

Evans, R. I., and B. F. Skinner. *The Man and His Ideas*. New York: Dutton, 1968.

Evarts, E. U. "Effects of Sleep and Waking on Activity of Single Units in the Unrestrained Cat." *The Nature of Sleep*. London: Churchill, 1961.Fagan, Joen, and Irma L. Shepherd. *Life Techniques in Gestalt Therapy*. New York: Harper & Row, 1970.

Fagan, Joen, and Irma L. Shepherd. *Gestalt Therapy Now*. New York: Harper & Row, 1971.

Faraday, Ann. *Dream Power*. New York: Berkley Publishing Corp., 1973.

Faraday, Ann. *The Dream Game*. New York: Harper & Row, 1974.

Featherstone, R. E., A. S. Fleming, and G. O. Ivy. "Plasticity in the Maternal Circuit: Effects of Experience and Partum Condition on Brain Astrocyte Number in Female Rats." *Behavior Neuroscience* 114, no. 1 (2000): 158-172.

Fedio, P., A. F. Mirshy, W. J. Smith, and D. Parry. "Reaction Time and EEG Activation in Normal and Schizophrenic Subjects." *Electroenceph. Clinical Neurophysiology* 13 (1961): 923-926.

Feinberg, Irwin, Richard Koresko, Fred Gotlieb, and Paul Wender. "Sleep Electroencephalographic and Eye Movement

Patterns in Schizophrenic Patients." *Comprehensive Psychiatry* 5 (1964): 44-53.

Fisher, Charles, Joseph V. Byrne, and Adele Edwards. "NREM andREM Nightmares," *Psychophysiology* 5, no. 2 (1968): 221-222.

Florin, Inger et al. "Screening of Tobacco Smoke Constituents for Mutagenicity Using the Ames' Test." *Toxicology* 18 (1980): 219-232.

Foulkes, David. "Dream Reports From Different Stages of Sleep." *Journal of Abnormal and Social Psychology* 65 (1962).

Foulkes, David. "Theories of Dream Formation and Recent Studies of Sleep Consciousness." *Psychological Bulletin* 62 (1964): 326-347.

Foulkes, David. *The Psychology of Sleep*. New York: Charles Scribner's sons, 1966.

Foulkes, David. "Children's Dreams: Age Changes and Sex Differences." *Waking & Sleeping* 1, no. 2 (1977): 171-174.

Foulkes, David, Ethel M. Swanson, and James D. Larson. "Dreams of the Preschool Child." *Psychophysiology* 5, no. 2 (1968): 220.

Foulkes, David, and G. Vogel. "Mental Activity at Sleep Onset." *Journal of Abnormal Psychology* 70 (1965): 231-243.

Foulkes, David, and G. Vogel. "The Current Status of Laboratory Dream Research, *Psychiatric Annals* 4, no. 7. (1974): 7-27.

Francher, Raymond E., and Robert F. Strahan. "Galvanic Skin Response and the Secondary Revision of Dreams: A

Partial Disconfirmation of Freud's Dream Theory." *Journal of Abnormal Psychology* 77, no. 3 (1971): 308-312.

Freud, Sigmund. *On Dreams*. New York: W. W. Norton & Co., 1952.

Freud, Sigmund. *Three Essays in the Theory of Sexuality*. New York: Aavon, 1962.

Freud, Sigmund. *An Autobiographical Study*. New York: W. W. Norton & Co., 1963.

Freud, Sigmund. *The Interpretation of Dreams*. New York: Avon Books, 1965.

Fromm, Erich. *The Forgotten Language*. New York: Grove Press, Inc., 1951.

Gage, F. H. "Brain, Repair Yourself." *Scientific American* 289, no. 3 (September 2003): 46-53.

Garfield, Patricia. *Creative Dreaming*. New York: Simon and Schuster, 1974.

Gellert, Shepard D. "How to Reach Early Scenes and Decisions by Dream Work." *Transactional Analysis Journal* 5, no. 4 (1975): 411-414.

Gentil, M., and M. Lader. "Dream Content and Daytime Attitude in Anxious and Calm Women." *Psychological Medicine* 8, no. 2 (1978): 297-304.

Gillham, Nicholas. *Genes, Chromosomes and Disease: from simple traits, to complex traits, to personalized medicine*. New Jersey: Pearson Education, 2011.

Giora, Zvi and Zohar Elam. "What a Dream Is." *British Journal of Medical Psychology* 47, no. 3 (1974): 283-383.

Glaubman, Hananyah, Israel Orbach, Orit Aviram, Irene Frieder, Meira Friedman, Odeda Pelled, and Rivka Glaubman. "REM Deprivation and Divergent Thinking." *Psychophysiology* 15, no. 1 (1978): 75-79.

Goldberg, Martin. "The Uses of Dreams in Conjoint Marital Therapy." *Journal of Sex & Marital Therapy* 1, no. 1(1974): 75-81.

Goodenough, Donald R., A. Shapiro, M. Holden, Chriber L. Steins. "A Comparison of 'Dreamers' and 'Nondreamers': Eye movements, Electroencephalograms, and the Recall of Dreams." *Journal of Abnormal and Social Psychology* 59 (1959): 295-302.

Goodenough, Donald, R., Herman Witkin, David Koulack, and Harvey Cohen. "The Effects of Stress Films on Dream Affect and on Respiration and Eye-Movement Activity." *Psychophysiology* 12, no. 3 (1975): 313-320.

Gordon, H. L. "A Comparative Study of Dreams and Responses to the Thematic Apperception Test." *Journal of Personality* 22 (1953): 243-253.

Gould, E., B.S. McEwen, P. Tanapat, L. A. Galea, and E. Fuchs. "Neurogenesis in the Dentate Gyrus of the Adult Tree Shrew is Regulated by Psychosocial Stress and NMDA Receptor Activation." *Journal of Neuroscience* 17 (1997): 2492-2498.

Guzman-Marin, R., N. Suntsva, M. Methippara, R. Greiffenstein, R. Szymusiak, D. McGinty. "Sleep Deprivation Suppresses Neurogenesis in the Adult Hippocampus of Rats. *European Journal of Neuroscience* 22 (2005): 2111-2116.

Hall, Calvin. *The Individual and His Dreams*. New American Library, 1972.

Han, M. E., K. H. Park, S. Y. Baek, B. S. Kim, J. B. Kim, H. J. Kim, and S. O. Oh. "Inhibitory Effects of Caffeine on Hippocampal Neurogenesis and Function." *Biochem Biophys Res Commun* 356 (2007): 976-980.

Hartmann, E. *The Biology of Dreaming*. Springfield: Charles C. Thomas, 1967.

Hartmann, Ernest, Frederick Baekeland, George Zwilling, and Patrick Hoy. "Sleep Need: How Much Sleep and What Kind?" *American Journal of Psychiatry* 127, no. 8 (1971): 1001-1008.

Hendricks, Marion N. "Experiencing in Dreams." PhD diss., University of Chicago, 1975.

Hiscock, Merrill & David B. Cohen. "Visual Imagery and Dream Recall." *Journal of Research in Personality* 7, no. 2 (1973): 179-188.

Hobson, J. Allan. "Sleep: Physiologic Aspects." *New England Journal of Medicine* 281, no. 24 (1969): 1343-1345.

Hobson, J. Allan, F. Goldfrank, and F. Snyder. "Respiration and Mental Activity in Sleep." *Journal of Psychiatric Research* 3 (1965): 79-90.Horne, J. A. "Hail Slow Wave Sleep: Goodbye REM." *Bulletin of the British Psychological Society* 29 (1976): 74-790.

Hume, K. I., and J. N. Mills. "Rhythms of REM and Slow-Wave Sleep in Subjects Living on Abnormal Time Schedules." *Waking & Sleeping* 1, no.3 (1977): 291-296.

Jersild, Arthur. "Child Development and the Curriculum." *Journal of Educational Psychology* 38 (1947).

Jiang W., Y. Zhang, L. Xiao, J. V. Cleemput, Bai G. Ji S-P, and X. Zhang. "Cannabinoids Promote Embryonic and Adult Hippocampus Neurogenesis and Produce Anxiolytic- and Antidepressant-like Effects." *Journal of Clinical Investigation* 115 (2005): 3104-3116

Johnson, L. C. "A Psychophysiology for All States." *Psychophysiology* 6 (1970): 501-516.

Jones, Richard M. *The New Psychology of Dreaming*. New York: The Viking Press, Inc., 1970.

Jourard, Sidney M. *The Transparent Self*. New York: D. Van Nostrand Co., 1971.

Jouvet, Michel. "The Paradox of Sleep: The Story of Dreaming." Massachusetts Institute of Technology, 2001.

Jung, C. G. *Modern Man in Search of a Soul*. New York: Harcourt, Brace & World, 1933.

Jung, C. G. *Psychology and Religion*. New Haven: Yale University Press, 1938.

Jung, C. G. *Memories, Dreams, Reflections*. New York: Vintage Books, 1965.

Jung, C. G. *Dreams*. Princeton: Princeton University Press, 1974.

Kahn, Edwin, Charles Fisher, Adele Edwards, and David Davis. *Mental Content of Stage 4 Night Terrors*, Proceedings of the 81st. Annual Convention of the American Psychological Association, Montreal, Canada, Vol. 8, (1973): 501-502.

Kamiya, J. *Behavioral and Physiological Concomitants of*

Dreaming, Progress report submitted to National Institute of Mental Health, 1962.

Karacan, I., A. L. Rosenbloom, and R. L. Williams. "The Clitoral Erection Cycle During Sleep." *Psychophysiology* 7, no. 2 (1970): 338.

Kempermann, G., H. G. Kuhn, F. H. Gage. "More Hippocampal Neurons in Adult Mice Living in an Enriched Environment." *Nature* 386 (1997): 493-495.

Kleim, J. A., K. Vij, D. H. Ballard, and W. T. Greenough. "Learning-Dependent Synaptic Modifications in the Cerebellar Cortex of the Adult Rat Persist for at Least Four Weeks." *The Journal of Neuroscience* 17 (1997): 717-721.

Klinger, E. *Structure and Function of Fantasy*. New York: Wiley, 1971.

Knowledge magazine, June 2010, 83.

Koob, Andrew. "The Root of Thought: Unlocking Glia - The Brain Cell that will Help us Sharpen Our Wits, Heal Injury and Treat Brain Disease." New Jersey, Pearson Education, Inc., published as FT Press, 2004.

Koulack, David. "Rapid Eye Movements and Visual Imagery During Sleep." *Psychological Bulletin* 78, no. 2 (1972): 155-158.

Krippner, Stanley, Michael Cavallo, and Richard Keenan. "Content Analysis Approach to Visual Scanning Theory in Dreams." *Perceptual & Motor Skills* 34, no. 1 (1972): 41-42.

Kroon, Hillevi Ruumet. "An Idiographic Study of Affective Interpersonal Relations in Waking Life and Recalled Dreams," PhD diss., Columbia University, 1972.

Lafenetre, P., O. Leske, Z. Ma-Hogemeie, A. Haghikia, Z.

Bichler, P. Wahle, and R. Heumann. "Exercise Can Rescue Recognition Memory Impairment in a Model with Reduced Adult Hippocampal Neurogenesis." *Front Behav Neurosci* 3 (2010): 34.

Latner, Joel. *The Gestalt Therapy Book.* New York: Bantam Books, Inc., 1974.

Levenson, Paul Neil. "A Study of the Relationship Between Dreams and the Waking State." PhD diss., New School for Social Research, 1974.

Lou, S., J. Liu, H. Chang, and P. Chen. "Hippocampal Neurogenesis and Gene Expression Depend on Exercise Intensity in Juvenile Rats." *Brain Research* 1210 (2008): 48-55.

Lowy, Samuel. *Foundations of Dream Interpretation.* London: Paul, Trench, Trubner, 1942.

Mak, G. K., E. K. Enwere, C. Gregg, T. Pakarainen, M. Poutanen, I. Huhtaniemi, S. Weiss. "Male Pheromone-Stimulated Neurogenesis in the Adult Female Brain: Possible Role in Mating Behavior." *Nature Neuroscience* (2007).

Malberg, J. E., A. J. Eisch, E. J. Nestler, and R. S. Duman. "Chronic Antidepressant Treatment Increases Neurogenesis in Adult Rat Hippocampus." *Journal Neuroscience* 20 (2000): 9104-9110.

Maron, L., A. Rechtschaffen, and E. A. Wolpert. "The Sleep Cycle During Napping." *Archives of General Psychiatry* 11 (1964): 503-508.

Mattoon, Mary Ann. *Applied Dream Analysis: A Jungian Approach.* Washington: V. H. Winston, 1978.

McCann, Joyce, and Bruce N. Ames. "Detection of Carcinogens as Mutagens in the Salmonella/Microsome Test:

Assay of 300 Chemicals: Discussion." *Proceedings of the National Academy of Sciences* USA 73 (1976): 950-954.

McLeester, Dick. *Welcome to the Magic theater*. Amherst: Food For Thought Publications, 1976.

Milunsky, Aubrey. *Your Genes, Your Health*. New York: Oxford University Press, 2012.

Mirescu, Christian & Elizabeth Gould. "Stress and Adult Neurogenesis." *Hippocampus* 16, no. 3 (2006): 233-238.

Mohapel, P., G. Leanza, M. Kokaia, and O. Lindvall. "Forebrain Acetylcholine regulates adult hippocampal neurogenesis and learning." *Neurobiology of Aging* 26 (2010): 939-946.

Monje, Michelle L., Shinichiro Mizumatsu, Shinichiro, John R. Fike, and Theo D. Palmer. "Irradiation Induces Neural Precursor-Cell Dysfunction." *Nat. Med.* 8, no. 9 (2002). http://www.medscape.com/viewarticle/442030.

Monroe, L. J. "Psychological and Physiological Differences Between Good and Bad Sleepers." PhD diss., University of Chicago, 1965.

Morris, Charles G., and Albert A. Maisto. *Understanding Psychology*, ninth edition. New Jersey: Person Education, Inc., Prentice Hall, 2010.

Mott, Francis J. "World Transformation," *Journal of Psychohistory* 4, no. 3 (1977): 319-335.

Nell, Renee. "The Use of Dreams in Couples' Group Therapy." *Journal of Family Counseling* 3, no. 2 (1975): 7-11.

Niedermeyer, E., and W. J. Lentz. "Dreaming in Non-REM Sleep: A Preliminary Study of Brief Diurnal Sleep in the Clinical EEG Laboratory." *Waking & Sleeping* 1 (1976): 49-51.

Noonan, Michelle A., Sarah E. Bulin, Dwain C. Fuller, and Amelia J. Eisch. "Reduction of Adult Hippocampal Neurogenesis Confers Vulnerability in an Animal Model of Cocaine Addiction." *The Journal of Neuroscience* 30, no. 1 (January 2010): 304-315.

Noone, Richard & Dennis Holman. *In Search of the Dream People*. New York: Morrow, 1972.

Olson, M. V., and A. Varki. "Sequencing the chimpanzee genome: insights into human evolution and disease." *Nature Review Genetics* 4 (2003): 20-28.

O'Nell, Carl W. *Dreams, Culture and the Individual*. San Francisco: Chandler and Sharp Publisher, Inc., 1976.

Paddock, C. "Study finds friends are genetically similar." *Medical News Today*, July 15, 2014. Retrieved from http://www.medicalnewstoday.com/articles/279595.php.

Palmer, T. D., A. R. Willhoite, F. H. Gage. "Vascular Niche for Adult." *Hippocampal Neurogenesis, J Comp Neurol* 425 (2000): 479-494.

Palmiere, L. "Intro-Extraversion as an Organizing Principle in Fantasy Production." *Journal of Analytical Psychology* 17 (1972): 116-136.

Passons, William R. *Gestalt Approaches in Counseling*. New York: Holt, Rinehart & Winston, 1975.

Patoine, Brenda. *What's New in Neurogenesis, An interview with Fred H Gage, Ph.D.* (n.d.) http://www.dana.org/news/publications/detail.aspx?id=6316.

Perkins, Bryan. "Chronic High Doses of Cannabinoids Promote Hippocampal Neurogenesis." Article from *Associated Content*, 2010.

Perls, Frederick S. *Gestalt Therapy Verbatim*. New York: Bantam Books, 1969a.

Perls, Frederick S. *In and Out of the Garbage Pail*. New York: Bantom Books, 1969b.

Perls, Frederick S. *The Gestalt Approach & Eye Witness to Therapy*. Ben Lomond: Science and Behavior Books, Inc., 1973.

Peterfreund, Emanuel & Jacob T. Schwartz. "The Phenomena of Sleep and Waking: A Unified Approach, *Psychological Issues* 7, no. 1-2 (1971): 243-287.

Pinker, Steven, Ph.D. *The Blank Slate: The Modern Denial of Human Nature*. New York: The Viking Press, Inc., 2002.

Polster, Erving and Miriam Polster. *Gestalt Therapy Integrated*. New York: Vintage Books, 1973.

Potter, Steven, Ph.D. *Designer Genes: A New Era in the Evolution of Man*. New York: Random House, Inc., 2010.

Prickaerts, J., G. Koopmans, A. Blokland, and A. Scheepens. "Learning and Adult Neurogenesis: Survival With or Without proliferation?" *Neurobioligy of Learning and Memory* 81 (2004): 1-11.

Ragueneau, Father Paul. *The Jesuit Relations and Allied Documents*. Vol. XXXIII, 77 Vols. New York: Pageant Book Co., 1959.

Randall, Alexander V. "Dream Sharing and Shared Metaphors in a Short Term Community." PhD diss., 1978

Rechtschaffen, Allen, Edward Wolpert, William Dament, Stephen Mitchell, and Charles Fisher. "Nocturnal Sleep of Narcoleptics." *Electroencephalography and Clinical Neurophysiology* 15 (1963): 599-609.

Rechtscchaffen, A. and P. Verdone. "Amount of Dreaming: Effect of Incentive, Adaption to Laboratory, and Individual Differences." *Perceptual and Motor Skills* 19 (1964): 947-958.

Rechtschaffen, A., G. Vogel, and G. Shaikun. "Interrelatedness of Mental Activity During Sleep." *Archives of General Psychiatry* 9 (1963): 536-547.

Reed, Henry. "Learning to Remember Dreams." *Journal of Humanistic Psychology* 13, no. 3 (1973): 33-48.Regush, June V. and Nicholas M. Regush. *Dream Worlds: The Complete Guide to Dreams and Dreaming.* New York: The American Library, Inc., 1977.

Reich, David E., and Eric S. Lander. "On the Allelic Spectrum of Human Disease." *Trends in Genetics* 17 (2001): 502-510.

Rogers, Carl R. *On Becoming a Person: A Therapists View of psychotherapy.* Boston, MA: Houghton Mifflin, Co., 1961.

Rogers, Carl R. *A Way of Being.* New York: Houghton Mifflin, Co., 1980.

Rogers, Carl R. *Client-Centered Therapy.* Constable, 2003.

Rosenblatt, Daniel. *The Gestalt Therapy Primer.* New York: Harper & Row, 1975.

Rosenzweig, M. R. "Experience, Memory, and the Brain." *American Psychologist* 39 (1984): 365-376.

Rosenzweig, M. R. "A Spects of the Search for Neural Mechanisms of Memory." *Annual Review of Psychology* 47 (1996): 1-32.

Ruifang, G., and P. Daning. "A Review of Studies of the Brain Plasticity." *Psychological Science* 28 (2005): 409-411.

Sabini, Meredith. "The Dream Group: A Community Mental

Health Proposal." PhD diss., California School of Professional Psychology, San Francisco, 1972.

Samuels, Arthur. "A T.A. Approach to Dreams." *Transactional Analysis Journal* 4, no. 3 (1974): 27-29.

Santarelli, L., M. Saxe, C. Gross, A. Surget, F. Battaglia, S. Dulawa, N. Weisstaub, J. Lee, R. Duman, O. Arancio, C. Belzung, and R. Hen. "Requirement of Hippocampal Neurogenesis for the Behavioral Effects of Antidepressants." *Science*, 2003, 301(805):809.

Sarason, S. B. Dreams and Thematic Apperception Test Stories, *Journal of Abnormal and Social Psychology* 39 (1944): 486-492.

Schachtel, Ernest G. *Iorphosis. On the Development of Affect, Perception, Attention and Memory*. New York: Basic Books, Inc., 1959.

Shepard, Martin. *Fritz: An Intimate Portrait of Fritz Perls and Gestalt Therapy*. New York: Saturday Review Press, 1975.

Shollar, Edward Robert. "Modifying the Sleep Cycle: The Effect of Pre-Sleep Instructions on the Length of Rapid Eye Movement Sleep Periods." PhD diss., New York University, 1975.

Shulman, Bernard. *Contributions to Individual Psychology: Selected Papers*, Alfred Adler Institute, 1973.

Simkin, James S. *Gestalt Therapy Mini-Lectures*. Millbrae: Celestial Arts, 1976.

Singer, J. L. and J. A. Antrobus. "A Factor Analytic Study of Daydreaming and Conceptually-Related Cognitive and Personality Variables." *Perceptual and Motor Skills* 17 (1963): 187-209.

Skinner, B. F. *Science and Human Behavior.* New York: Free Press, 1953.

Skinner, B. F. *Verbal Behavior.* New York: Appleton, 1957.

Skinner, B. F. *Contingencies of Reinforcement.* New York: Appleton, 1969.

Skinner, B. F. *Cumulative Record.* 3rd. ed. New York: Appleton, 1972.

Skinner, B. F. *About Behaviorism.* New York: Knopf, 1974.

Smith Edward W. L. ed. *The Growing Edge of Gestalt Therapy.* Secuacuse: Citadel Press, 1977.

Starker, Steven. "Daydreaming Styles and Nocturnal Dreaming." *Journal of Abnormal Psychology* 83, no. 1 (1974): 52-55.

Starker, Steven. "Daydreaming Styles and Nocturnal Dreaming: Further Observations." *Perceptual and Motor Skills* 45 (1977): 411-418.

Starker, S. and R. Hasenfeld. "Daydream Styles and Sleep Disturbance." *Journal of Nervous and Mental Disease* 161 (1976): 313-317.

Stephey, M. J. "What Happens When We Die?" *Time* magazine, 2010.Stevens, John O. *Gestalt Is.* New York: Bantam Books, Inc., 1977.

Stewart, Kilton. *Pygmies and Dream Giants.* New York: Joanna Colter Books, 1976.

Sykes, Bryan. *DNA USA: A Genetic Portrait of America.* New York: W. W. Norton & Co., 2012.

Takkouche, Bahi, Mahyar Etminan, and Agustin Montes-Martinez. "Personal Use of Hair Dyes and Risk of Ca;ncer: A

Meta-Analysis." *Journal of the American Medical Association* 293 (2005).

Tart, Charles, ed. *Altered States of Consciousness*. New York: Doubleday, 1972.

Thomas, Rosanne M., and Daniel A. Peterson. *A Neurogenic Theory of Depression Gains Momentum* (2010). http://molinterv.aspetjournals.org/content/3/8/441.full.

Tylor, Edward B. *Researches into Early History of Mankind and the Development of Civilization*. New York: Henry Holt and Co., 1978.

Van de Castle and Peter Hauri. "Psychophysiological Correlates of NREM Mentation." *Psychophysiology* 7, no. 2 (1970): 330.

Van Praag, H., X. Zhao, and F. H. Gage. "Neurogenesis in the Adult Mammalian Brain. In M. S. Gassaniga (Ed)." *The Cognitive Neurosciences*. Third edition. Cambridge, MA: MIT Press, 2004.

Van Praag, H., T. Shubert, C. Zhao, and F. H. Gage. "Exercise Enhances Learning and Hippocampal Neurogenesis in Aged Mice." *The Journal of Neuroscience* 25 (2005): 8680-8685.

Vogel, Gerald. "Studies in Psychophysiology of Dreams, III. The Dream of Narcolepsy." *Archives of General Psychiatry* 3 (1960): 421-428.

Walker, Priscilla C. "The Hypnotic Dreams: A Reconceptualization." *American Journal of Clinical Hypnosis* 16, no. 4 (1974): 246-255.

Wallin, David Jefferey. "Intentional Dreaming: An Active Approach to the Imagery of Sleep." PhD diss., The Wright Institute, 1977.

Wan, J., H. Zheng, Z.-L. Chen, H.-L. Xiao, Z.-J. Shen, and G.-M. Zhou. "Preferential Regeneration of Photoreceptor From Muller Glia After Retinal Degeneration in Adult Rat." *Vision Research* 48 (2008): 223-234.

Ward, Charles D., Karen M. Ward, Susan B. Randers-Pehrsen, and Linda Runion. "Birth Order and Dreams." *Journal of Social Psychology* 90, no. 1 (1973): 155-156.

Watson, James D. and Andrew Berry. *DNA: The Secret of Life*. New York: Random House, Inc., Audio Publishing Group, 2003.

Watson, J. B., and R. Rayner. "Conditioned emotional reactions." *Journal of Experimental Psychology* 3 (1920): 1-14.

Weiner, B. "Effects of Motivation on the Availability and Retrieval of Memory Traces." *Psychological Bulletin* 65, (1966): 24-37.

Wells, Spencer. "Deep Ancestry: Inside the Genographic Project." Washington, D.C., National Geographic Society, 2006.

Wentz Christian T., and Sanjay S. P. Magavi. "Caffeine Alters Proliferation of Neuronal Pecursors in the Adult Hippocampus." *Neuropharmacology* 56, no. 6-7 (May-June 2009): 994-1000.

Whiteman, H. "People tend to choose partners with similar DNA, study suggests." *Medical News Today*, May 25, 2014. Retrieved from http://www.medicalnewstoday.com/articles/2777291.php.

Wicklund, June Baehler. "The Use of Modeling to Elicit Dream Recall as a Preparation for Psychotherapy." PhD diss., Northwestern University, 1976.

Wong, E. Y., and J. Herbert. "Circulating Corticosterone Inhibits Neuronal Differentiation of Progenitor Cells in the Adult Hippocampus." *Neuroscience* 137, no. 1 (2006): 83-92.

Yong, Ed. "Did sex with Neanderthals and Denisovans shape our immune systems? The jury's still out." *Discover* Magazine, August 27, 2011.

Zim, Shraga. "Cognitive Development of Children's Dreams. PhD diss., Yeshiva University, 2011.

Zimmer, Carl. "The Brain: The Dark Matter of the Human Brain." *Discover* Magazine, Sept. 2009.

Zimmerman, John T., Johann M. Stoyva, and Martin L. Reite. "Spatially Rearranged Vision and REM sleep: A Lack of Effect." *Biological Psychiatry* 13, no. 3 (1978): 301-316.

Zimmerman, W. "Psychological and Physiological Differences Between "Light" and "Deep" Sleepers." PhD diss., University of Chicago, 1967.

Zinker, Joseph. *Creative Process in Gestalt Therapy*. New York: Vintage Books, 1978.

www.ingramcontent.com/pod-product-compliance
Lightning Source LLC
Chambersburg PA
CBHW020758160426
43192CB00006B/365